Creation of Lifestyle

Architecture

BARBADIAN HOUSE

Michael E. Jordan

AuthorHouse™ LLC
1663 Liberty Drive
Bloomington, IN 47403
www.authorhouse.com
Phone: 1-800-839-8640

Published by AuthorHouse 02/28/2014

ISBN: 978-1-4918-6386-2 (sc)
ISBN: 978-1-4918-6488-3 (e)

Library of Congress Control Number: 2014902008

CREATION OF LIFESTYLE

Architecture

Architect
MICHAEL E. JORDAN, BA. (HONS.) ARCH, RA, ASSOC. UKA, BIA

Principal of the Technical Evening Institute

Acknowledgments

Many thanks to Mrs. Adeline Sparman, who assisted with the first draft; Senator Professor Emeritus, Dr. Henry Fraser, GCM, and Dr. Ron Hercules, both of whom edited the first draft; my assistant, Ms. Alana Edwards, who edited and formatted the final manuscript; photographer, Mr. Felix Kerr, for the beautiful photographs displayed throughout the book as well as the joyful experiences we had around the island; and noted historian, Mr. Morris Greenidge, for his particular insight and historical acumen, as well as his encouragement.

Additional thanks to the owners and occupants who maintained the houses photographed and shown as examples of the vernacular architectural heritage of our island, Barbados.

M. E. J.

CONTENTS

Foreword

I am honoured and delighted to be invited by Michael Jordan to write a foreword to his important work *Creation of Lifestyle* on Architecture. This publication comes at a time when Barbadians in particular, but I suspect Caribbean people in general, have become direly frustrated by what I would euphemistically term 'the inexactness of house building'.

As a student, he observed and discussed classical architectural sites in Italy, which equip him with a direct sense of Design for our region based on the English influence but also bearing the Roman and Greek traditions and styles in mind. Michael's avocation as a teacher as well as his training and experiences as an architect, equip him admirably to pass on his knowledge by way of this book.

It is my fervent wish that anyone with an interest in understanding Architecture–anyone with a hope of building in the future, and any prospective or current student of Architecture–will make the small investment to own this book. For it offers a sure pathway out of the pitfalls of building, but it also illuminates some of the dark corners in our understanding of the splendid but varied types of architecture which form an integral part of the Heritage of Our Islands.

My sincerest congratulations to Michael for this thoughtful contribution to our knowledge base. In addition, my very best wishes for the success of this timely publication.

Morris Greenidge
Author: *Holetown Barbados, Settlement Revisited and other Accounts*
       St Mary's Church – a History
       Bridgetown, Barbados – a Walking tour in six parts.

Preface

This publication seeks to engage readers, students (future and current) of architecture and others with the subject of lifestyle and its connection to good, satisfying architecture. It will also enlighten individuals whose intent is to build their personal dream house as to how integral their lifestyle should be to its design. Readers are completely drawn into a fresh and more accurate perspective of what makes successful architecture. For example, Historic Bridgetown and its Garrison—as well as the National Trust Open House programme— provide a clear illustration of the link between Barbadian vernacular and the classical European tradition in architectural design. It is quite normal for the public to pass by and stare, or sometimes, have the opportunity to look more closely at the some of the historic houses that are part of our Heritage, but how often do Barbadians consider the functionality of those structures? How relevant they were to their times and how adaptable are they to modern living?

Richard Ligon, whose observations of life in Barbados in the early days of Settlement, wrote *"A True and Exact History of Barbados"* for which he is revered, but few people know that Ligon was the architect behind the building of the famous Holborn House which was built in 1660, and was demolished in 1960 to make way for the Bunker storage of the Deep Water Harbour. His design of Holborn was an almost temperamental outburst against the former practice of the day, as they *'never consider which way they build the houses— they just get them up—which is why so many of them are so insufferably hot.'*

It is this writer's hope that Readers will be able to connect the Heritage architecture to modern living, but will also be able to have a clearer notion of how a well-planned and produced structure can itself be completely functional, aesthetic but also, in the near future, be a considered part of our Built Heritage.

Introduction

The creation of lifestyle is quite interesting since most people have the desire to create their own dream house, but often have reservations due to the belief that their budgets may be inadequate as high-quality materials usually cost an arm and a leg. My solution for this is that, in many instances, high-quality materials can be visually imitated and durable enough for the life expectancy of a building. Additionally, volumetric spacing and sequencing of movement are of utmost importance and, if thematically decorated (i.e. similar to setting a theatrical stage), can create excitement and drama.

The seven elements that I consider the basis of architectural design from my perspective—prestige, value added, intimate appeal, etc—is discussed with respect to lifestyle in this text. The History of Barbadian Architecture acknowledges the fact, since the influences of the colonial buildings of the Georgian period were a precursor to historic Bridgetown and its Garrison in Barbados with the historical elements of Barbadian (Bajan) vernacular structures.

'Some Types of Local Houses' and **'Other Architectural Projects'** are chapters which discuss the various designs with connecting indoor/outdoor living space and shaded patios, as shown in ***single-plan*** type at Carmichael and Brighton in St. George, and a proposed ***three bay-plan*** type called "HAZA" located in St. Thomas.

'Art, Science and Design of Building; A Sketching Look at Architecture' consists of a three-part article series by the author, originally published in the October 1994 edition of a local daily newspaper – the Barbados Advocate. Based on a Hilton Seminar, these articles explain some aspects of architecture to the public.

Finally, this book also mentions the Architectural Design course, developed by the author, which assisted a number of students in preparing portfolios of their work for interviews to gain University entry as well as to work as draughtsmen in preparing planning applications.

Chapter 1

HISTORY OF ARCHITECTURE

Barbados, an island in the Caribbean (seen in Fig.1), was claimed in 1625 by the English under John Powell who accidentally landed, during a severe storm, while en route from a trading voyage to Brazil. They took the island in the name of James I, King of England. On his return to the UK, Powell reported this to his employer, William Courteen.

On 17th February 1627, Courteen's expeditionary ship—**William and John** under Captain Henry Powell and with eighty persons (including 10 Africans) on board—landed at Holetown in Barbados.

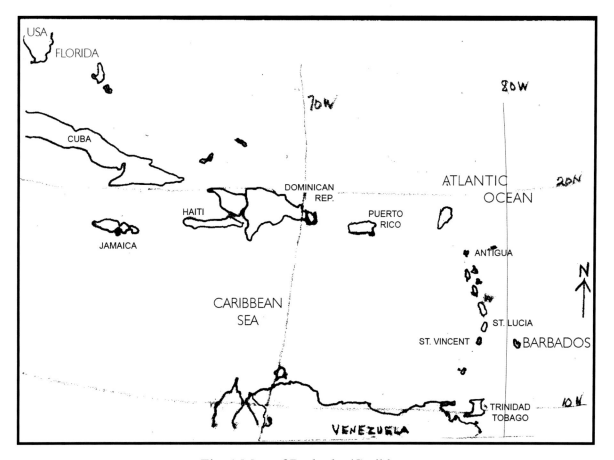

Fig. 1 Map of Barbados/Caribbean

A second group of settlers soon followed them, since the island was granted also to the Earl of Carlisle. In July 1628, fifty settlers belonging to the RAWDON Syndicate of merchants, under the auspices of James Hay (Earl of Carlisle) landed on the inlet close to the Indian Bridge, subsequently known as Bridgetown, capital of Barbados.

By then the population of the Holetown group, in 1628, was approximately 1600. A civil War between the two factions soon ensued and the Bridgetown faction overtook, by subterfuge, the Holetown settlers and eventually confiscated their possessions, which included nearly all of the lands stretching from Sandy Lane to the tip of Saint Lucy in the north and eastwards towards the coast of Saint Andrew. After the initial spasms of settlement, with the help of 32 contracted Surinamese Amerindians, life continued with the cultivation of major export crops such as indigo, cotton and tobacco in addition to food crops such as yams, cassava, plantains, sugar cane and corn but their export crops did not produce lucrative results for long as the same crops were being produced in the new colonies of America but by more efficient means.

Around 1640, a Dutchman, called Pieter Brewer, experimented with sugar cane, which had been originally brought to the island in 1627 from Brazil, but was used only as a food energy source for the workers. By 1645 the first commercial sugar crop was produced. Large scale sugar manufacture began under settlers such as the Holdipp Family and under the Draxes who still retain major sugar lands in Barbados to this day.

The next major event was Oliver Cromwell's victory over the Monarchy in England and the subsequent execution of King Charles I. As a result, many Royalists escaped or sent to Barbados as prisoners. By 1650, there was much disagreement between the two factions of settlers. On one side were the Royalists whilst on the other, the Cromwell supporters were growing in number. This situation manifested the exact diverse conditions existing in England.

In 1652, after a six month futile stand off between Proprietor Lord Willoughby of Parham, the Royalist Governor, and Cromwell's Admiral Sir George Ayscue (who had been sent to wrest Barbados from the Royalists) a truce was reached and the **Declaration of Barbados** (Treaty of Oistins) was agreed. This agreement admitted Sir George Ayscue as governor but allowed the Royalists to retain most of their holdings, and also allowed them the right to a say in the government of the island (No taxation without representation)—something like the "Magna Carta" in England.

In 1780, the island was devastated by a very destructive hurricane, which forced many planters to leave for England and some went off to South Carolina in the United States of America. Many of the houses, of all types, were destroyed, necessitating massive rebuilding.

A second, similarly devastating hurricane hit the island in 1831. This caused even more damage, this time more structural than agricultural. Many newly built churches were lost.

The Architecture of the first European settlers in Barbados was a reflection of the British tradition. Almost none of it survives, but later houses like Nicholas Abbey, Drax Hall House, Brighton and Warrens Great Houses point to an opulent but ordered lifestyle brought straight across the Atlantic from the English county manor to the sugar plantations of Barbados whose geographical position, 100 miles East of the Caribbean Chain of Islands, located it as the first port of call from both Europe and Africa.

Many of the major structures which survived the 1831 hurricane were the military buildings which subsequently influenced the architecture of the island.

The Barbados Museum & Historical Society

The military built forts along the West and South coasts - from modern day Atlantic Shores to Harrison Point—with major installations at Needham Point, Holetown, Speightstown, and had their main complex, called the Garrison, at St. Ann's Fort. Its main guardhouse (built in 1804) is located more or less a mile south of Bridgetown.

Most of the Barracks were built in the late 18th century, in the familiar military model of arcades, built of previously disregarded ballast bricks. Note the classical details in its Clock Tower and pediment, bearing the Arms of William IV at the Garrison Main Guard.

The Plantation Houses, slave huts and Bajan chattel houses use many adaptations from these influential Garrison buildings.

I would now like to show the influence on the Bajan vernacular architecture by looking at some of the historic houses of Barbados as highlighted by the National Trust of Barbados.

St. Nicholas Abbey

Drax Hall

The first Settlers of Barbados were the nomadic Arawaks who lived in huts made of wattle and daub; others lived in caves long before 1627 but, even though early English cartographers show us their walking trails, their living existence was in virtual denial and, of course, their architecture comes to us only in the form of unearthed artefacts and petroglyphs in caves, not by permanent structures.

By 1651, Britain was already enforcing the precursor to the Navigation Act (1707), which protected the British Interest by discouraging other countries' ships from visiting Barbados to carry out trade

In 1655, Barbados was therefore blocked from carrying out material trade with the Dutch but this could not stop the transmission of ideas and Customs. By that time, a very great house, known as Nicholas Abbey, was built using the Dutch gable ends and chimney breast based on an English house plan with parapet walls. Colonel Drax soon built another Dutch style Great House, known as Drax Hall (1660). In Bridgetown, there was Nicholls House of smaller but similar influence in design.

In 1657, a brilliant Englishman, Richard Ligon, who was fascinated by the lifestyle and home life of Barbados, published the book ***"A True and Exact History of Barbados"*** and became manager at Kendal Plantation in the parish of St. John. He had quite a bit to say (see Preface) of the architecture of his day.

In 1700, wealthy Quakers built Harmony Hall just east of the Roebuck, probably. It was a single house containing a portico entrance with wide verandahs. Its original roof replaced with a Bajan style parapet roof after the 1780 hurricane. Note the reference to the Garrison buildings (originally soldiers' barracks) with the Georgian and "Palladian motifs". In the 1750's, crofters' huts (now known as slave huts) were built by and for the second class English and Scottish former indentured labourers who had risen in rank on the plantations. These built of coral or rubble stone with a hipped roof and low ceilings. After Emancipation, most of the whites either migrated or moved to the east coast of the island, leaving their houses to be occupied by aspiring blacks, mostly the new class of field-gang leaders or "drivers". Black artisans simply copied this very functional design using timber as the source material, hence the proliferation of the 4 Hip house alongside the even more pleasing timber gabled house.

The destruction of Architecture in Barbados, like all other major countries around the world, has been due primarily to the loss of faith in the original mythical beliefs expressed in the use of *load bearing* construction. The introduction of scientific reasoning therefore lead to a shift in Architectural thought. Its emphasis was once on humanist values (such as emotions and poetic expressions), but now focuses on scientific fact, necessity and function expressed in the use of *post and lintel* construction.

Farley Hill

In Barbados, before the Second World War, very few black people could afford to build a stone house far less to talk about Architectural content and character. Although the historic houses of Barbados built without university-trained architects, many of the plans copied from England, Holland or America. These projects built with the labour of local, black artisans, under the authority of very powerful and wealthy, white men who had been briefly educated in England. As England holds the library of the world knowledge, black people built to emulate their masters' homes and display their status to their community, with this concept firmly in mind.

A similar attitude was expressed by English people during the reign of King George IV, as seen in the book ***"Small Georgian Houses and their details (1750–1820)"*** by Stanley C. Ramsey & J. D. M. Harvey: February 1975, page 27 paragraph 2 which states: *"The distinguishing trait of most of these late Georgian houses is a sense of order and proportion. There is a wonderful variety in their design, evidencing a wealth of invention and fertility of imagination which is only possible when the canons and fundamentals of an art are frankly accepted."*

I believe what they are talking about is "Typology" and closure of the limits of Architecture. This adherence to "Typology" was the hallmark of our Barbadian vernacular architecture, from the slave hut to the plantation great houses, illustrated below in *Table 1: Similar Lifestyles–Similar Plans–Varied Social Levels.*

However, please bear in mind that the Second World War (1939–45) combined with Hurricane Janet (1955) depleted the ranks of first class artisans in Barbados. Many went to the Armed forces of Britain and Canada, and, after the completion of the War, England whose labour force was severely depleted (250,000 men lost in Battle) needed to rebuild its battered and war-torn infrastructure. She attracted all types of Artisans from Barbados so that when Janet hit, we witnessed a new type of construction with the double flat roof, used in wood as well as stone houses, a far quicker and easier structure to build, and new but perfectly understandable terminology in the name 'Storm-carpenter"—a succinct description of *'necessity being the father of invention'.*

Michael E. Jordan

(**TABLE 1:** SIMILAR LIFESTYLES - SIMILAR PLANS - VARIED SOCIAL LEVELS)

	Working Class	Middle Class	Plantation
Wraparound Patio	BECKELL'S ROAD	WORTHING	BUCKLEY
Georgian/Wraparound	INDIAN POND	HARMONY HALL	THE GARRISON
Verandah to Wrap around Patio	DAYRELL'S ROAD	SPOONER'S HILL	BELLEVILLE
Verandah	BRITTON'S CROSS ROAD	BANK HALL	BAGATELLE

After the 1972 Town Planning Order, along with the Independence of Barbados in 1966, a new age began. Clients who were about to build homes were told that there was a shortage of good artisans and good timber so they opted for concrete block structures instead of using coral stone structures. They installed six feet wide aluminium and glass windows and glass doors of four feet wide under the guise of durability. For the verandah, concrete column used without any order, with the verandah enclosed with decoration blocks of any shape.

This free license in the making of Architecture broke the Typological language of building, so that we have neither 'fish nor fowl', and a unique, not so pleasant hybrid is created.

This destruction can be curtailed if Jalousie doors and windows were on sale in stores. We now have the stone Quarry at St. Philip with machinery to cut stone into manageable sizes at comparatively low cost.

It is the hope of the author that people of the Caribbean will once again embrace our heritage and the art of our vernacular architecture.

Since the Town Planning Act of 1972, the need to submit applications for the proposed construction of all developments has had a devastating effect on the character of Bajan Vernacular Architecture, though the Town Planning Act set out to assist the Environment through the regulation of building, maintaining of road reserves, minimum side distances and height of buildings. Along with these Town Planning acts are the Ministry of Health laws, which in principle try to provide our buildings with good ventilation, height and damp proofing for adequate habitation.

The reason for the destruction of our Architecture is due to a shortage of artisans skilled in building heritage style houses as well as the low wages paid to construction workers. New home-owners' lack of cultural awareness is suggested by the "American look" of many recently built houses.

Many uninformed owners seem to prefer the international look over the "Bajan Style". Maybe this reminds some of us of the bad experience of Colonialism and thereby a memory of slavery, which we all would like to forget. What we fail to recognize is that the heritage buildings were a solution to the problems of our environment. Our low, squat buildings with wide verandahs and Jalousie louvered doors and windows can be incorporated into all our Architectural projects. Some recent projects substantiate this fact as seen below.

Forde House

Bajan Chattel House

Artisans who are now trained at the Polytechnic should be paid as much as - or more than - some white collar workers; the bad legacy of "Plantation Society" should be phased out. See the book ***"Persistent Poverty"*** by George L. Beckford: Oxford Press 1972, chapter 3, page 83 last paragraph which states:

"The basic problem goes much deeper than this. The nature of social and political arrangements created several biases toward a continuous state of under development. Inherent social instability impedes investment, the rapid pattern of social, economic and political power prevents the emergence of a highly motivated population and racial discrimination inhibits the fullest use of the society's human resources."

Exemplary Virtues of Bajan Vernacular Architecture (as hand-crafted building construction)

Some of the exemplary virtues of our Vernacular Architecture are:

1) WIDE VERANDAHS - for shade and ventilation
2) TIMBER HAND-RAIL - hand-crafted and lightweight for gallery
3) HIGH PITCHED ROOF - (at least 35 degrees pitch) with gable-end, fixed wind vented louvers
4) JALOUSIE WINDOWS AND DOORS
5) PARAPET WALLS - to prevent lifting of eve ends during hurricane winds
6) THICK SOFT STONE WALLS - to reduce heat gain on the building fabric
7) RAISED FLOOR LEVELS - to prevent flooding in low lying areas, to give the building more prominence and to help prevent rising dampness and better breeze into the house.
8) ORIENTATION OF THE BUILDING - to take advantage of the North East Trade winds in order to situate enclosed rooms away from the South West sun side of the building.

Exemplary Virtues of Classical Architecture (as mythological building construction)

These virtues of exemplary Classical Architecture as the articulation of the basic elements in construction are:

1) FLOORS – external emphasis indicating the point of separation between the floor and wall
2) COLUMNS – Ionic, Doric and Corinthian orders (base, shaft, capital)
3) ENCLOSED WALLS (stone/brick) with doors and windows–frames embellished with architraves
4) POST AND BEAM - a type of construction combining columns and beams articulated as architraves
5) PEDIMENT – usually a triangular construction consisting of architraves, frieze and cornice
6) GEORGIAN MOTIF – an architectural style generally consisting of a pediment situated in the centre of a façade with articulation of ground, middle and top floors as well as positioning doors and windows in the centre of column spacing.
7) ROOFS – these are usually Gable, Hip, Lean-to (Shed roof)

Chapter 3

ART, SCIENCE AND DESIGN OF BUILDING SKETCHING LOOK AT ARCHITECTURE
(Barbados Advocate, October 1994 in three parts)

PART ONE

Michael Jordan has been a qualified architect since 1984. He holds a Bachelor's Degree in Architecture from the Polytechnic of Central London, now the University of Westminster.
In this first of a three-part series, Jordan examines and explains some aspects of architecture.

There is very little talk about architecture and environmental design in our country today. In a continuing effort to extend Total Quality Architectural design in this business community, we are offering a programme which will enlighten many directors and persons who are interested in this subject.

From my experience in preparing architectural design, many clients ask architects for a plan while others would also provide a sketch showing their wishes. The sketch would give me some very vague ideas of the user's requirements. It is at this stage that the architect's input would be offered in formalizing a brief and trying to bring some measure of architectural content to the project.

Sometimes, if the architect is not careful, this exercise could lead to misunderstandings since many clients do not appreciate how they can gain architecture out of a simple set of subjects and a modest budget.

There is an old adage that states *"people hear what they see"* and since the architect's studio may not be a great architectural space, many people do not expect great architecture. So begins the arduous task of trying to educate and bring some additional architectural value to clients.

Let us now look at what is Architecture and Architectural Design.

Two sides

Architecture is the art and science of building. It embraces the building strongly and well, and also beautifully so as to produce pleasurable emotions in those who behold the building. Thus, there is a material side to architecture as well as an aesthetic side. The material side is expressed in the construction of walls, floors, roofs, doors and window openings, etc. The aesthetic side is shown in such matters as the expression of purpose, good proportions, appropriate arrangement of parts and the application of taste and artistic skill to every feature of the building.

Architectural design is the process of creating a building; that is, of arranging its various parts so that they will best accomplish the purpose for which the building is to be used, and clothing the building so that it satisfies the taste and gives pleasure to the beholder. The designing of a building is done graphically by the use of paper, pencils, colours and drawing instruments. The design is shown in the form of plans, elevations, sections and perspective views.

Architectural design and architectural composition are practically the same things. In designing a building, an architect may use any available materials and methods of construction, as well as any details of ornament that he/she thinks will produce the best and most pleasing results.

Site Appraisal

The first task performed is to visit the site for a site appraisal. This includes:

1. **Breeze direction** – This is an attempt for cross ventilation and to achieve appropriate air changes required for comfort.
2. **Sun travel from sunrise to sunset** – The kitchen and morning rooms are built to the east for morning sunlight and to shade the house from the hot afternoon sun with the use of patios, wide overhangs, bathrooms, storerooms, garages and the use of trees to provide shade for the buildings.
3. **Best view** – Patios and large windows are placed to the advantage of the best view and some rooms extend into borrowed space beyond so that one feels they've gained this outside space as theirs.
4. **Historical significance** – The use of historical significance is to capture and pay some respect to the heritage of the present environment. Take the colour and materials used and the method of construction and style of the buildings.
5. **Topography** – This is the various slopes of the land which may result in the building being split level or having a full basement.
6. **Town and Country Planning requirements** – Usually a minimum building distance from the centre line of the road and a minimum side distance of 6 feet from the boundary line.

7. **Ministry of Health** – The Ministry requires a minimum window size to suit the size and usage of the room, which would result in getting air changes per minute in the room.

8. **Estimated budget** - The average building rate ranges from $200 per square foot for the average house to $600 per square foot for executive houses due mainly to material finishes. The maximum building size can be worked out to suit the client's budget.

9. **Parking** – This determines the appropriate space for vehicles to park, exit or enter the property as well as a turning bay (a space which allows for vehicles to turn around safely).

10. **Context** – This consists of situating the house or structure in alignment with the neighbours and conforming to the neighbourhood. Or even more simply, it's the construction of the building in relation to the environs.

11. **Accommodation** – This is the number of rooms desired which comprises the building within a given budget.

Full Services

The standard procedure followed by an architect is listed in the following stages:

Stage A: **Taking a brief** – This is the concept of the project and the number of rooms required by the client.

Stage B: **Feasibility study** – this entails an analysis of the size of the house and whether the client's requirements can fit the client's budget.

Stage C: **Design sketches** – These are presented to the client for comments and adjustments and then final plans are made and prepared for submission to the Town and Country Planning and the Ministry of Health.

Stage D: **Town and Country Planning Application** – Six copies of the plans, one copy of the Surveyor's Plot and a $100 application fee is required. There is then a four to six month waiting period before approval from the statutory boards before the next stage.

Stage E: **Working drawings** – These are required to give directions to the builder and to formulate a contract between the builder and set legal standards.

The list for the working drawings of an average sized house is as follows:

1. Site and Location
2. Floor Plan
3. Elevations
4. Foundation Plans
5. Electrical Plan
6. Section
7. Roof Plan
8. Ceiling Plan
9. Door Schedule
10. Window Schedule
11. Bedroom Cupboards
12. Bathroom Details
13. Kitchen Details
14. Entrance Gate
15. Wrought Iron Details
16. Miscellaneous Details
17. Programme

Stage F: **Bill of Quantities** - A listing of the materials with or without the Prices.

Stages G & F: **Tenders and Contracts** – This entails at least three prices for each of the trades and formulating contracts with the various sub-contractors.

***Stages J & K*: Site operations** – After the tenders have been accepted and the contracts signed, work is mobilized on the site.

The duties of the architect include the management of the building contracts, fort-nightly visits to the site to check the progress and quality of the work. The architect also conducts site meetings, produces progress reports and instructions, etc. In addition, a monthly Interim Certificate for the contractors' payments must be produced.

***Stage L*: Certificates** – After the project is completed, the architect signs the Certificate of Partial Possession and the Certificate of Practical Completion when the client takes over the project.

***Stage M*: Feedback** – After the defects liability period, the architect then issues the final certificate (The Certificate of Satisfactory Completion).

<u>Freely above need</u>

"Mere need does not give rise to beauty, nor does every accidental utilitarian factor have to be taken into account to endow something with character, otherwise chaos results. Only someone who moves freely above (material) need will be capable of beauty, provided that in his freedom he still endows the object with the characteristic aspect that makes it individual." – **K. F. Schinkel, *"Karl Friedrich Schinkel: A Universal Man"*, p. 50**

The architecture of the project can be determined by the proposed lifestyle of the client since the environment created by the design sustains the client's wishes.

Let me explain further, since this is a very important area that is overlooked and misunderstood. For example, if a client wanted to create a tropical environment, the design may allow for large openings, court yards, pools and other vernacular motifs such as jalousie doors and windows and wide verandas. The additional use of soft stone is encouraged because of its ability to breathe and not hold heat.

Rooms may have high ceilings which may be conical, tray or flat, depending on the interior design and the emotional content to be created. Therefore, an architect can contrive any environment which is a kind of stage set.

And finally, the sequencing and route of these different volumetric shapes of these various spaces all come together to produce a very rewarding experience.

"By rendering construction mythically fictive classical thought posits reality in a contemplative state, wins over the depredations of petty life and in a moment of rare disinterestedness, rejoices in sacramental power it has over contingent life and nature." – **D. Porphyrios, AD 52 5-6 1982, p. 57**

THE STATE OF ARCHITECTURE

PART TWO

The state of architecture in Barbados today is adopting the North American ideology with wide expanses of glass (to gain an indoor outdoor environment), arch and long rectangular sash windows and the roofs are gabbled and hipped.

They are moving away from the Bajan Bungalow with one roof built during the early 1930s; the houses around the 1980s and beyond have many different roofs. Additionally, there is the use of some Bajan vernacular motifs, for example, window hoods. Moving indoors, one may notice the open plan concept incorporating the use of indoor planting, which is opposite to the concept of the traditional rooms as boxes.

The reintroduction of colours such as beige and cream and other pastel shades makes the house seem calmer and cooler. The colour green is not only related to the natural foliage but it blends with the flora when used to paint the trimmings. Another contrasting method to the traditional painting of the house is that home owners are turning to trowel plastic for their exterior finishes.

There is a shift from the traditional building system where each family got a contractor to build the house up until the mid '70s. The new trend is now speculative built homes ready for sale from a choice of two to three types.

There is a re-emergence of the use of hard woods such as purple and green heart with only a few pitch pine houses being built for the low income earners. I think this a tragedy since these timber houses are built following the line of the Bajan square box bungalow. I believe the same material and size can be designed to produce more architectural content.

The middle-income house in the heights, parks and terraces are beginning to have some very interesting elevational treatment; the streamlining of many different roofs, the use of asphalt shingle roofs, bay windows, french doors and wide patios all produce a cottage-like effect. This segmenting of the façade is a reflection of the care and pride which the Barbadian takes in his home.

Many of these bungalows at a cursory glance seem to be extended family homes, but upon entering the home one is deluded to find the accommodation is no more than a three-bedroom two-bathroom house. From my analysis, the problem seems to be a conflict due to a misunderstanding of the need to gain comfort from the actual dimensions of the building.

Some years ago in the U.K., this problem was addressed in London to achieve minimum standards, and the Essex Design Guide was formulated, but to follow slavishly a prescribed dimension to my mind is a mistake.

In Barbados there seems to be some predilection on the client's part to request 12 feet rooms, six-foot patios and three-feet-wide corridors.

If a project is composed using these prescriptions, this leads many clients not qualifying for mortgages due to oversized designs and in many instances only qualifying after exhaustive revisions. Another indictment on many houses is the use of double garage spaces at the front of an otherwise beautiful house, thereby creating a travesty.

Outside space

Regarding the siting on a small plot of land, not enough thought is sometimes given to the outside space and the house ends up in the centre of the lot, and the remaining space cannot be extended upon without breaking the Town Planning building requirements.

In this case, the house could have been sited to one side, leaving a positive space on the other side. An architect can successfully address a small plot in ways that are aesthetically pleasing.

In the 1990s, there has been a tremendous improvement to most completed projects due to the input of hard and soft landscape architecture and better site planning.

The built environment of the public and commercial sector is very attractive and well landscaped with the use of vernacular motifs and traditional colour. The end result is very pleasing and conducive to total quality production and the work ethic.

I believe this is because most of these large projects are done by professionals and the clients having set out a brief for a specific corporate image, work in close conjunction with the professional, thereby producing a successfully pleasing environment.

Performance evaluation

Included in an architect's duties is performance evaluation. In evaluating the contractor's performance, the architect plays two distinct roles:

(i) Inspector – Where required by the contractor, the architect must check certain work is in absolute accordance with the contract documents.

(ii) Judge – Other clauses of the Standard Form require the architect to provide a qualitative opinion on work, which is not specifically stated in the contract documents. The clauses imposing this duty are phrased "to the architect's satisfaction".

In order to fulfil these duties, certain powers are granted to the architect by the Standard Form including:

(a) The ordering of tests to be made on goods, materials or workmanship.

(b) Requiring proof of compliance of goods or materials with the contract documents.

Training

Year 1, 2, 3 – The seven-year course in architecture begins with the first degree (3 years). Subjects studied are Perception and Communication. This includes philosophy, psychology, art history, workshop practice, cultural experiences, painting, music, literature and long essays.

Dissertations were to be presented on all the topics covered, the actual drawings being the minor part.

The last of the first degree study was history and theory. This was the Origins of Architectural Form, the First Enlightenment. It entailed 19th and 20th century theory and production, social and economic conditions of building, economics, sociology, business management (politics and religion), history and theory of ideas (enlightenment, empiricism, historical idealism, romanticism, phenomenological aesthetics, structuralism and the epistemology of the sign), history of aesthetics and new ideas along with the future.

Practical attachment

Year 4 – At the end of the first degree, the student does a year of practical attachment with a professional office.

Year 5 – The third part of the training (2 years) covered the technical studies aspect, which was: strength of materials, emotional content of lighting and air-conditioning, building comfort, building law, building contracts, building regulations, city planning, building failures, building reports, in the use of the building, history of the building, technology and technical design parameters.

Year 7 – After the post graduate studies, the student takes the final professional exam at the end of the seventh year, some architects work a few years with a firm of consultants before going on their own, or some stay in the public service and others go into teaching and writing books. Some architects prefer to stick to litigation and arbitration with their biggest portfolio being party wall cases in terrace housing.

ARCHITECTURAL ENCOUNTERS

PART THREE

Having graduated from Combermere and the Technical Institute in 1969 with level passes in Building and Engineering (Geometrical) Drawings, my interest in architecture took me by a stroke of luck to work for Tomlin Associates (architect of the Queen Elizabeth Hospital and the Government Headquarters), where I experienced my first encounter with great architecture.

The Captain was real humanist architect and touched all who came in contact with him, with his warmth and passion for great architecture. Like a true captain, he worked long hours, sometimes Peggy (his wife) had to literally take him off the board. I admired Tommy (as he was affectionately known) and decided to follow in his footsteps.

Drake House was the turning point. It had a picnic dining room, a swimming pool and "V" jointed timber bay windows, and all the patio was at the back of the court-yard. I was shocked by the positioning of this patio but was soon colonized to the idea of privacy and intimacy. It was here that my appetite was whetted and I started my long quest for the secrets and joys of architecture.

I began drawing house plans and making blue print copies in the mid-70s and Captain Tomlin came around to give me his blessings.

The first project he passed on to me I wanted to show him that I could walk in his footsteps and not let him down since he was accustomed to placing full confidence in anyone he gave a task. The project was Gollop House and both he and the client were very pleased with my work.

The next project I did was the family home. In this design, I endowed the project with tropical architecture and it is now bathed in shrubbery.

Dissatisfied

After working for six years, I became dissatisfied doing town planning applications only. I spoke with the Captain and he gave me letters of reference and loaded with my portfolio, I flew off to London. The tutors and my fellow students were very kind to me and I gained my Honors Degree in Architecture. Part of my training took me out to Vienna where I saw in the "flesh" the works of the great masters like Sempler, Michangelo and Hansen. The work seemed to be designed for immortals. The buildings seemed so perfectly proportioned as if nothing could be added or subtracted except for the worse.

I have returned home and I am working on a number of middle-income homes and I try to infuse some of these benefits of great design, but find myself blocked with some clients' limited passion for architecture whose are the interface.

Since beauty cannot be transferred from person to person, we can communicate to educate on another by communicating metaphorically.

Our mind is not free if it is not the master of its imagination; the freedom of the mind is manifest in every victory over self, every resistance to external enticements, every elimination of an obstacle to this goal, every moment of freedom is blessed.

I both wish and feel obliged to devote my art to ennobling "all human conditions" by perfecting man morally through aesthetic education and in this way enabling him to humanize his relationships.

Every work of art must incorporate an entirely new element, even if it is created in a well-known, beautiful style. Without this new element, it cannot fully arouse the interest either of the artist or the viewer. Yet, this new element is what engages his interest in the world as it exists, highlighting the extraordinary quality of existence and thus suffusing existence with a new colour, flooding it with the charm of a vital spirit.

My recent work has developed along the lines of Classical and Bajan Vernacular architecture, since I have a predilection for the emotional content and philosophy of the values of the classical sensibilities. Classical architecture is based on mimetic elaboration of vernacular building tectonics and the mimetic reflection of human senses (like using sign language, or like an actor performing for an audience). By rendering construction mythically fictive, classical thought posits reality in a contemplative state, wins over the depredations of petty life, and in a moment of rare disinterestedness, rejoices in the sacramental power it has over contingent life and nature.

Let me explain further; what distinguishes a shed from a temple is its mythological power. The temple possesses construction that is used to give artistic meaning and communication of feelings and nature. The base of a column can be seen as the foot, the shaft as the body and the capital as the head.

The experience of load bearing is perceptible through the bulging in the shaft or on the other hand, to a modernist using geometry and not feelings. The tree trunk although not smooth is rendered as a perfect cylinder. A pediment can be used to say entry or another example is a pergola with wines on top can be seen as a grove of trees.

The basic elements of building, according to J-N-L Durand (a professor of l'École polytechnique), is the point (the column), the line (the wall), the plan (the floor). The basic typology of spaces are the *stoa* (school corridor), the atrium (a building with a central courtyard opened to the sky), the *megaron* (the hall).

Juggling act

The composition of a building is like the composition of a choir, where different voices combine to form an ensemble. For example, having acquired the proposed brief from the client, the composition is a precarious juggling act—to balance the queries and desires on one hand to the perception and priorities of the architect on the other—to get inside the heads of two different people and then to put them both on the same tract.

Where I find the problem lies is in the lack of understanding of the profession of what is an architect and architecture. Very often clients give architects a set of utilitarian requirements but seldom add the artistic content and proposed environment they would like to achieve. In compensation for this, they take the architect to see a friend's home or a magazine, which is their way of communicating inner expressions. I organised the Hilton seminar to give a discourse on the subject with guest speaker Liam O'Connor R.I.B.A., London Designer of the Bomber Command Memorial, Hyde Park, London, England.

Below is an example of the steps clients are required to go through in conjunction with the architect to achieve success and smooth management of the building processes and procedures:

Orientation
Architectural Services
Inception
to
Completion

24 Months Ensures Quality

The Future is being created by Imagination, Vision and Perseverance.

Client Procedure

1. Decide to **buy land** to build.
2. Save 10% to **Deposit** on land.
3. Show the Land to the Architect.
4. **The Brief**:-
   Lifestyle e.g. (Family retreat in a Tropical Landscape, or House to Rent, etc).
   Accommodation: Guest room,

   3 Bedroom, 2 Bathroom, to suit the Budget.

5. Client will approve Architect's **Sketch** with minor changes

6. Client to apply for a **Mortgage**.
   Documents required:-
   - 1/3 Salary & Job Letter
   - **Life Insurance** to cover Mortgage
   - Approved T.C.P.O Plan
   - Contractors Estimate
   - **Q**uantity Surveyors Valuation
   - Negotiation Fee
   - Commitment Fee
   - Attorney's Fee to prepare Mortgage
   - Show a Credit Rating of 18 Points
7. After the Mortgage is approved the Client will receive **a Letter** (not money).
8. Apply for a **Bridging Loan** at a Bank (use the Mortgage Letter as security).

Architect Procedure

   –
   –
   –

1. Take **Brief** and a (**Fee 0.5%**) from the Client
2. **Visit** the Site, prepare Feasibility Study and a **Sketch.** (*Delivery time 1 month*).
3. Client /Architect meeting to present the Sketch.
4. Take Fee (1%) from the Client to complete **Stage C.**
5. Architect to prepare **T.C.P.O. & M.O.H.** applications.
6. Submit T.C.P.O & M.O.H Application, Drawings # 1-3 (Receive 2% Fees) (*6 mths*). **(Stage D&E)**
7. Prepare **Working Drawings** # 4 -15 Specifications & Building Codes (Receive **3%** Fees). (*2 mths*)
8. Send out information to 3 Contractors & Sub-Contractors (for **Tenders**) receive 1% Fee. (*1 mth*)
9. Client / Architect meeting to OPEN TENDERS. **(Stage F&G)**
10. Send out letters to inform the Tenders of the outcome and **select** a Contractor.

9. Choose the Contractor (from the **3 Tenders**) whom the Architect has presented.

10. Attend **Commissioning Meeting** to pay **Mobilization Fee** to the Contractor (and Sign **the Contract Document**) to assure Quality.

11. Attend **monthly Site Meetings** along with the Contractor and the Principal parties (chaired by The Architect), Client will pay Contractor the Draw-Down according to the Interim Certificate prepared by the Architect (Get the **monthly Draw-Down** from the Bridging Loan Funds).

12. **Receive the keys** to the Project (Architect to deliver Completion Certificate).

13. After living in the Project (house) for **3** months let the Client prepare a **Snag List** (the defects), the Contractor repairs the defects/Snags.

14. Pay the balance (5%) to the Contractor to get the Architect to give him **The Final Certificate** on completion of the works.

15. The Architect will apply to T.C.P.O. to get the **Certificate of Compliance** (**C** *of* **C**).

16. Client will present **C** *of* **C** to their Attorney At-Law, to complete the Mortgage (Mortgage Company will **pay off the Bridging Loan** and **Hold the house as Security**).

11. Architect / Client and Contractor Meet to sign Contracts & Drawings to Mobilize **the Works** (receive 2.5% Fee). (*6 mths*)

12. **Monthly Site Meetings (Stage K):-**
    To prepare:
    1. Interim Certificate (to get Draw-Down).
    2. Progress Report.
    3. Check quality of the Works.

13. At Completion of the Project, prepare a **Completion Certificate** for the Client and get from the Town Planning Office, the **Compliance Certificate**, to be delivered to the Attorney-At-Law representing the Mortgage Company, to expedite the Mortgage transfer. **(Stage L)**

14. Prepare the **Snag List** for the Contractor to make good all "Snags"/Defects.

15. Pay the Contractor the final 3-5% held in accordance With the Contract (for the Snags / repairs) which occurred during the **Defects Liability Period.**

16. Issue Copies of the **"Final Certificate"** to the Contractor and the Client.

Certification

At prescribed stages in the construction programme the architect is empowered to check the work completed to date. If the work is to his satisfaction, the architect may then issue and Interim Certificate to be sent to the contractor, with copies for the quantity surveyor, the employer and the file. Great care should be exercised before issuing any certificate.

Site visits

Periodical site visits should be made by the architect and the intervals will depend upon a number of factors, including:

a) Type and complexity of the project
b) Nature of the employer
c) Personal knowledge of the contractor
d) Locality of the site
e) Whether or not a clerk of works is employed
f) Particular events, for example, the arrival of equipment
g) Unforeseen events, for example, bad weather
h) The stage of the work reached.

On arrival, the architect should inform the site supervisor of his presence, and deal with only him or his representative during the visit. A record should be kept of all site visits, noting any observations, information supplied and actions to be taken. A copy of the record may then be sent to the quantity surveyor.

In conclusion, I hope this brief explanation of client and architect would go towards the better understanding of client architect relations, so the architect would be challenged to produce more pleasing projects and a sustainable environment.

*"Art sets up a world; art sets forth the earth." - **Heidegger**.*

Project planning and implementation duration

I would like to advise prospective clients about the time taken to produce a building from inception to completion.

<u>Outline plan of work</u>

Small Works Contract

Formulating the brief (clients requirements)	1 week
Site Appraisal (feasibility study report)	4 weeks
Design and Planning Application	16-24 weeks
Mortgage Finance	8 weeks
A set of working drawings	8 weeks
Bills of Quantities	8 weeks
Tenders and Contracts	4 weeks

Site Operation (building programme)	24–30 weeks
TOTAL	87 weeks

N.B.: See Table 2: Process and Procedures in Appendix

Building cost

The average building rate (popular finishes lower to middle income homes) is approximately $200 per square foot [year 2005].

Mortgage Finance

Normal pay-back period 15-25 years. The mortgagee needs to be gainfully employed and be bankable. (The client must pass the mortgage finance test with a score of not less that 18 points)

N.B.: The monthly repayment of the loan is about one third of the salary

Bridging loan

This is a short-term lending arrangement (overdraft) to construct a project until completion, at which stage the project will be transferred to a mortgage finance company (long-term lenders).

Throughout my discussion about architectural design, I have sought to solicit the central themes of what is /ought to be the exemplary virtues of good design. I have stressed the practical and emotional consequences of these themes.

For as one explores their implications, they draw us toward the goal of action and practical reason, they lead us to the Total Quality of culture—culture alone *"tames the freedom of the will without stifling it"*.

Chapter 4

SOME ARCHITECTURAL PROJECTS BY MICHAEL E. JORDAN

I have acquired a vast amount of experience and knowledge by working in a number of varying companies as well as by studying and travelling in pursuit of my love for the art of architecture; I am a talented architect.

My love for architecture is easy to see when you start to speak with me on the subject. I have a special love for the classics due to their timeless values. I am very much involved in educating persons in the beauty, importance and benefits of architecture in their lives. This love for architecture extends into my love for landscaping, which, for me, does not pre-exist the other—*"the idea of extending the inside to outside rooms"*. For me, **Architecture is the art of creating a <u>specific lifestyle</u> using building construction to create the required environment.**

There are seven benefits of architecture, from my perception:
1) Value added
2) Prestige
3) Intimate appeal
4) A legacy of values
5) Dramatic sequencing of spaces
6) Good cross-ventilation
7) A self-improved mind

IDEAL LIFE
- o Client's brief
- o Client's budget
- o Site Appraisal (see page 20)
- o Architectural References
- o My experience in the practice of architecture
- o My personal love for the classics due to its timeless values
- o My love for landscaping, the idea of extending inside rooms to outside rooms, that is landscaping

- o The idea of typology in correlation to building structure and the creation of lifestyle
- o Respect for the building code, town planning rules and regulations, the Ministry of Health and the Ministry of Transport and Works

HOMES DESIGNED BY MICHAEL E. JORDAN

<u>Home in Carmichael Heights, St. George, built-1986</u>

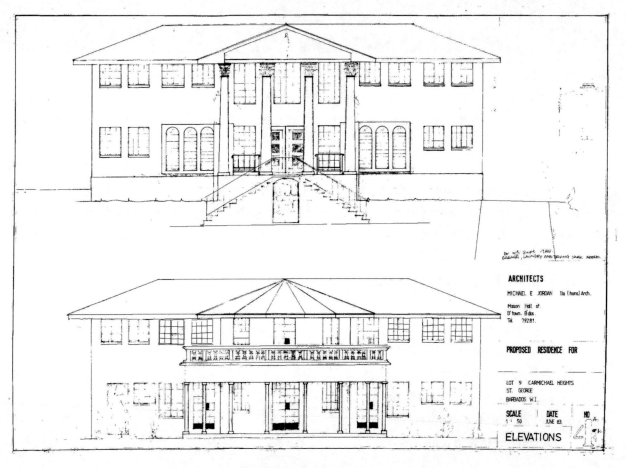

Front/Back Elevation

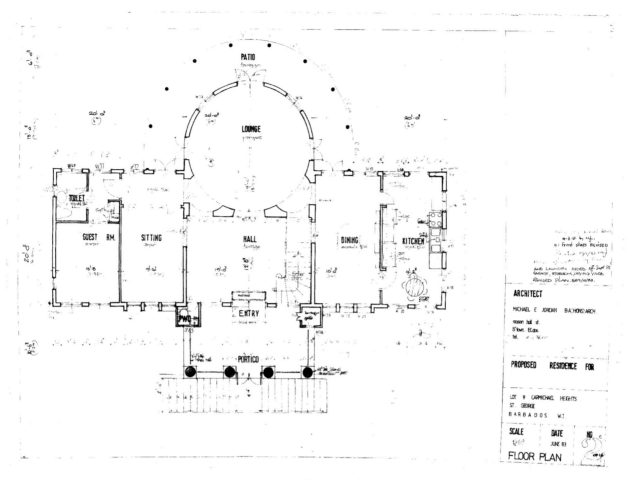

Ground Floor Plan

This private dwelling in St. George (built 1986) was conceived in 1983 while on a train from Vienna, where architectural students went on our study tour to Vienna. I met a fellow Barbadian on the train. He was well groomed and he walked and spoke with a sense of measured tranquillity. Subsequently, I did a site visit in Barbados. The magic of the site is its panoramic views to Bridgetown and the country on the north-eastern side. My client made a sketch of four strokes and an equilateral triangle on top. Immediately, I knew the rest of the story- classicism, order, history and traditional architecture.

The house is designed on a platform known in roman culture as a *piano Nobile* due to the topography of the site. This opportunity recalled a staircase at the Altes Museum in Germany, built in 1825.

Altes Museum

Designed by the celebrated German architect, K. F. Schinkel (1781-1841), this grand staircase leads to a portico of a giant Corinthian order (simplified) forming the centrepiece. The fluted columns are constructed using concave arices (which we had to plaster with added white lime to avoid failure). Moving into the double height lobby, a mahogany staircase leads to a circular family room.

The Entrance Hall

Its conical ceiling is made of tongue and groove pitch pine boarding with a hardwood finial from which a chandelier hangs. Off the family room is a semi-circular deck for country side viewing. On the left of the family room is the master bedroom suite and two other rooms on the other side.

The plan is a single depth, laid out in a cruciform. This typology allows good cross ventilation flooded with natural daylight. But, even more precious is the direct access to the flower gardens. This project is dramatic and delightful with quiet serenity.

'Haza': A Home in St. Thomas

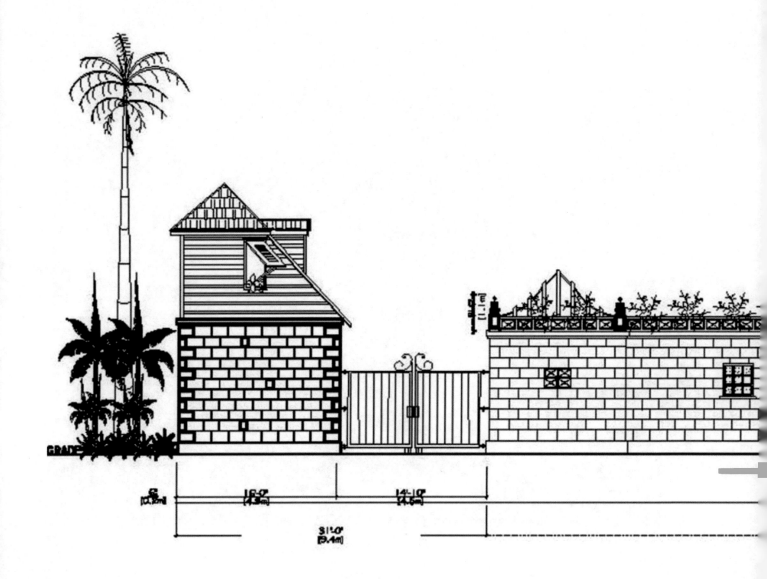

West Elevation

Haza: a private residence in St Thomas, Barbados set on two acres of land sloping down to a ravine which springs from Mt. Hillaby, St. Thomas. It wraps around the site, passes under Bridge Road, St. Michael and ends in the careenage in Bridgetown. This design was challenging because I had many options but had to *count the cost.* My idea is to **create a lifestyle of noble simplicity and quiet grandeur** due to my architectural studies in London, the study tour to Vienna, as well as Villa D'este in Rome and the open house programme sponsored by the Barbados National Trust, particularly the all inspiring Maddox by Oliver Messel, the famous British stage set designer. I accepted the challenge due to my affinity for indoor/outdoor lifestyle, the concept of imitation of nature (*a building is not merely a wall structure; when the physical model is designed, this built environment acts as a metaphor for social lifestyle*) as

West Elevation

well as growing up in Barbados surrounded by Georgian and vernacular architecture. At Heron Bay, on the west coast of Barbados, I like the grandeur of double height space which accommodates a grand staircase. However, the Italian master, Andrea Palladio (1508–1580), often hid stairs in his own stairwells as in Venice at the Villa ROTUNDA, Villa PISANI and other projects. In 1987, the British architect, Quinlan Terry, designed Oak Farm, in Kentucky, U.S.A. as well.

Michael E. Jordan

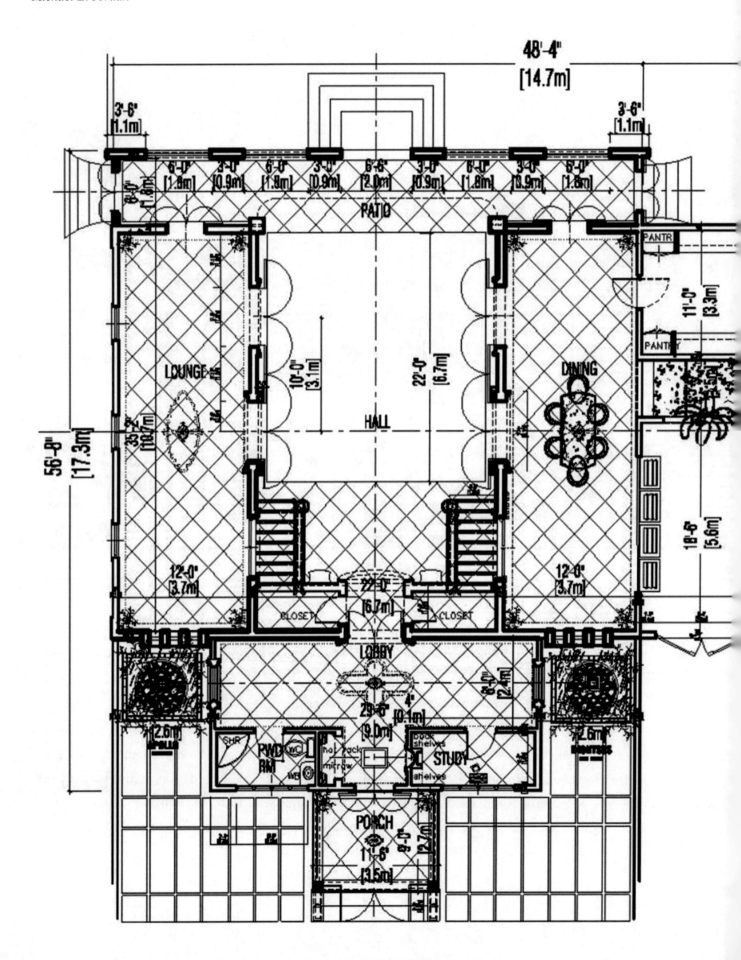

34

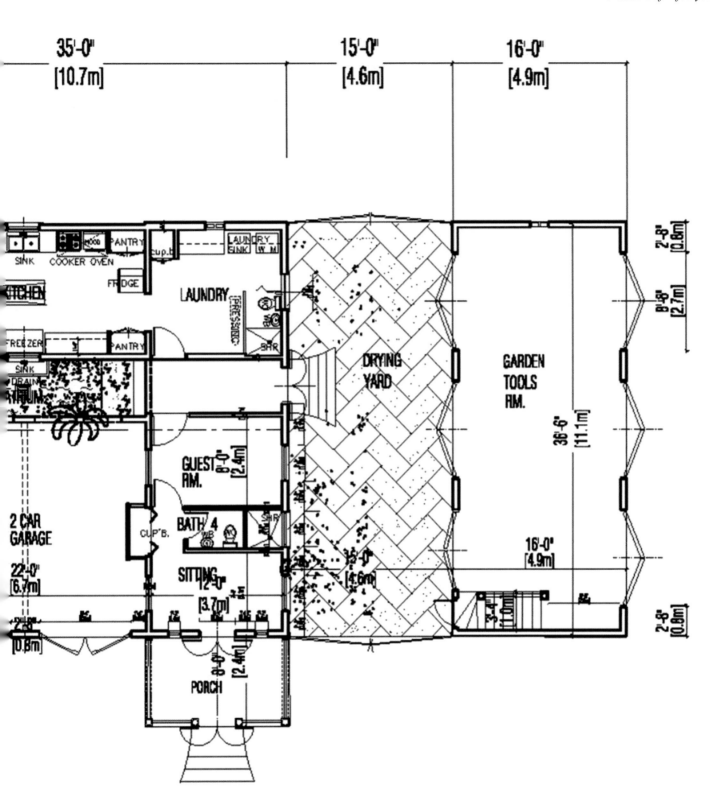

GROUND FLOOR PLAN
4690 sq ft.(469m2)

Ground Floor Plan

At Haza, the staircase is celebrated for dramatic effect. One enters the house through a walled and fountain courtyard, furnished with an Ionic Pergola, covered with hanging patria vines. By laying coral stone pavers on geometrical pathways, like a Greek cross, this footpath will control the visitors' movements. So, this enclosure edits out the known world. Finally, there's a sense of melancholy and privacy. On arrival at the porch/chamber two turned hardwood columns and two Acroteria welcome one to the porch/chamber, inside the chamber where one is received at the jalousie front door and invited into the lobby where you are introduced to a bust of **Equiano** which is secured in a Coral Stone Niche. A few steps into the lobby look right and left, through large elliptical windows. Fortunately, rock gardens come into view, containing statues of Apollo and Dionysus.

Before a dramatic entry through the Doric arch—which leads to the semi-outdoor, double height great hall—one enjoys the paintings, family portraits, a moulded centrepiece and architectural renderings decorating this lobby to inspire refined conversation. The element of surprise is both exciting and theatrical when moving from the shade of the lobby to the magnificent, semi-outdoor hall architecturally designed with a cathedral ceiling, and an Ionic proscenium arch, coral stone cornices, architraves, and skirting details. Here, Michael will pursue his love for ballroom dancing. [He's *a qualified ballroom dance teacher, an Associate member of the United Kingdom alliance, of Blackpool, England…*].

Three jalousie/lattice doors on the flanks create symmetry but the hierarchy of the central Doric portal is symbolically embellished with 'blocked' Coral Stones and Architraves, this portal is crowned with a broken Pediment to guard the Acroterium, here, one enters the principal room at Haza. The gratia lounge is decorated with Biedermeier furniture, oil paintings, a chandelier and a plaster moulded centrepiece.

At last, one is captivated by the awesome wonder and majesty of this special room. Back to the great hall the familiar geometrical theme of the Greek cross is repeated, naturally the dining room on the opposite side mirrors the space of the gratia lounge. This repetition reminds one of the 4x4 timing of a foxtrot dance or a Shakespearian sonnet. Inside the dining room a few steps away from the coral stone picnic/dining table there is an orchid atrium to separate the service wing from the main house. The kitchen, laundry, garage, maid's room and the drying yard which separates the garden tool shed from the kitchen.

Back to the indoor/outdoor great hall on the main axis, there is a panoramic view of Bridgetown and Carlisle Bay framed with coconut trees. In the foreground a Hex-style patio flows onto the swimming-pool terrace where guests can socialize.

Michael E. Jordan

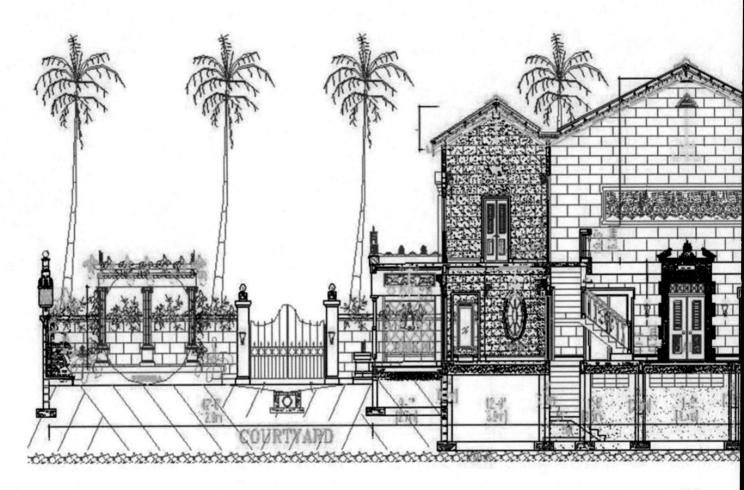

COURTYARD

`HAZA`

~~ARCHITECT~~ ~~MESSRS~~ ~~H. MESSRS~~(son) ~~SETH~~

17C

LONG. SECT

Long Section

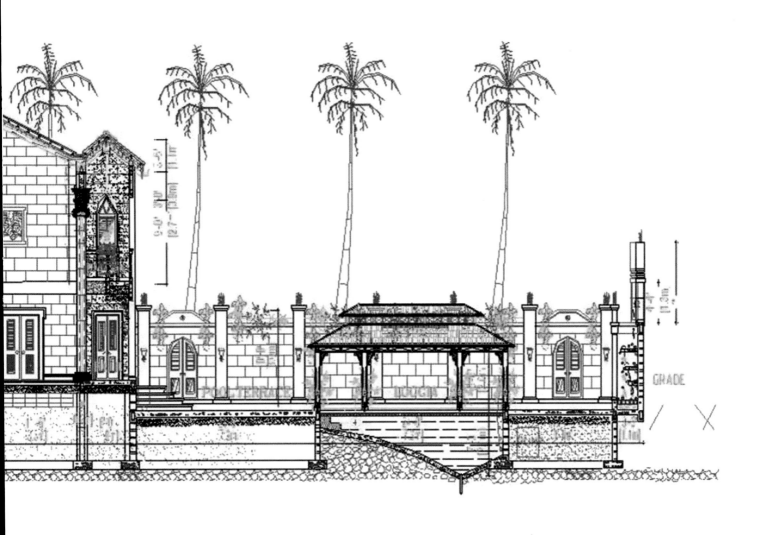

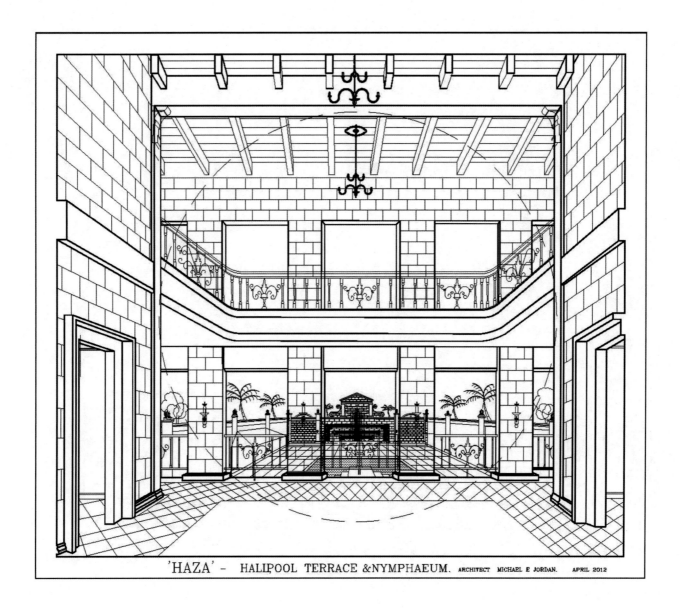

'HAZA' - HALIPOOL TERRACE &NYMPHAEUM. ARCHITECT MICHAEL E JORDAN. APRIL 2012

The Hall

In this palatial hall the mood is unmistakably serene. The room at the top of the double staircase is theatrically designed; one penetrates an arched portal to enter this gallery/pavilion. Flanking the portal two full height windows open to the magnificent hall. Doors at the end of this wall lead to the bedrooms. On each short side of this gallery central doors lead to royal carriage—like balconies, on the eastern wall three full height jalousie windows capture the rising sun and the north-east trade winds. All eight openings are fitted with jalousie doors or full height Louvre windows to experience airy all-around panoramic views. Looking eastward we view the coral stone courtyard furnished with an Ionic Pergola and the Memorial fountain.

Everyone will enjoy this view of the tropical country-side. Looking south is the Grantley Adams International Airport. Looking westward through the proscenium arch of the great hall the stage is set in anticipation for a drama by placing the swimming pool, and the Nymphaeum on centre stage with Bridgetown, the sea and the sky as the backdrop. Turn ninety degrees to the north there is a view of the driveway off the main road with Cave Hill in the background. After watching the movie titled *'Gifted Hands'*, guests take their final glass of champagne while Michael leaves for the master bedroom suite on the south wing. Sometime later, guests will retire to two rooms on the west wing where they enjoy a private veranda.

There is a sense of security inside the main house which is a single volume size at 24ft x 48ft x 48ft sheltered with gable roofs of zinc sheeting, block walls are plastered and rendered to imitate coral stone. Flood lighting outside, chandeliers and candle lighting in the hall, gratia lounge and the dining room. Chandeliers, reading lamps in the bedrooms and family room, concealed lighting in the atrium and courtyards. Candle-lights on the pillars smother their edges to create intimacy on this romantic patio. Finally, there is general lighting in all other rooms.

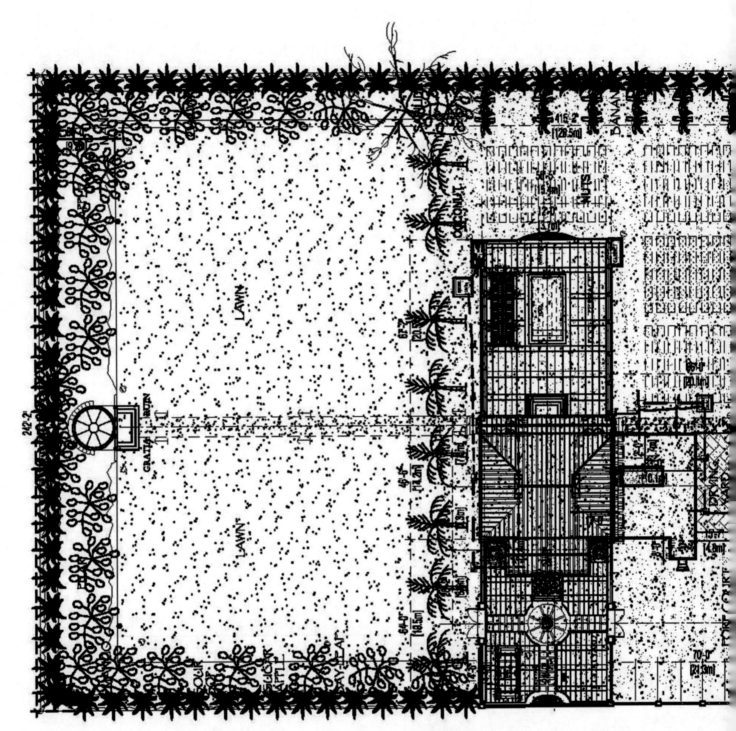

ARCHITECT - MICHAEL E. JORDAN ;BA (HONS);ARCH ;RA ; ASSOC.RICA; BIA.

Site Plan

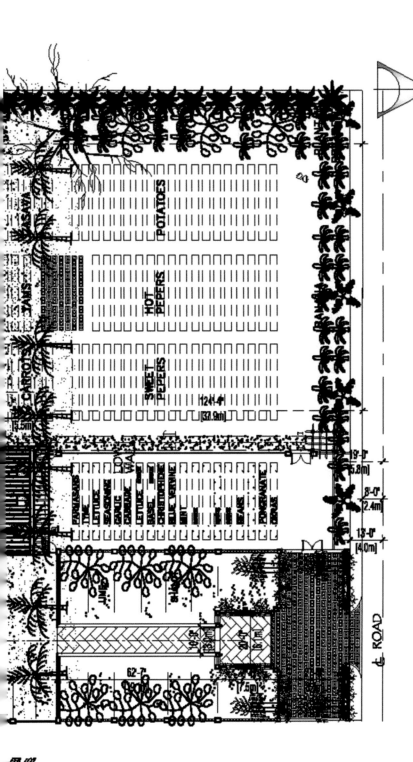

The landscaping thus places the building as a sandwich between Royal palm and fruit trees laid out in perspective lines to create an avenue which forms a shaft of space to focus towards Bridgetown and the countryside. On the lawn, there is a hatchery strategically placed on a north-south axis, which passes through the patio and terminates at the gratia ruin on the edge of the orchard, at the north-west quadrant is the kitchen garden. In another quarter, there is a private herb garden.

"Life in this reclusive world is absolutely beautiful; it's a place of noble simplicity and quiet grandeur created to enjoy the benevolent gift of life.

And there was light."

'HEPHZIBAH': A Home in St. George, built 2001.

The design of a private residence for a lady in the St. George valley, located a stone's throw away from St Luke's Anglican Church, had to be handled delicately since the narrow north-south site slopes up from the road and enjoys an awesome view to south ridge. The planning requirements dictated that we build a narrow plan house congruent with the plot. After the site analysis a strategy was conceived to edit out the neighbourhood thereby placing the house in its own context, resulting in the impression of a larger domain. Excavating the sloping rock formed a level pad for the building to rest itself. To site the building back from the road created a deep driveway, allowing time to enjoy the landscape before entering a walled forecourt located on the west side leading to the garage.

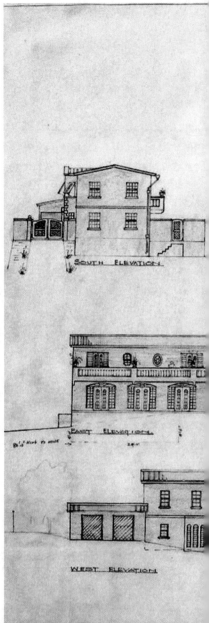

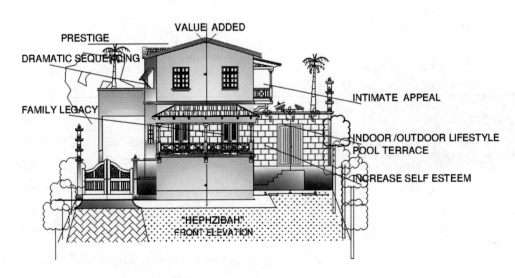

Front Elevation (showing seven benefits)

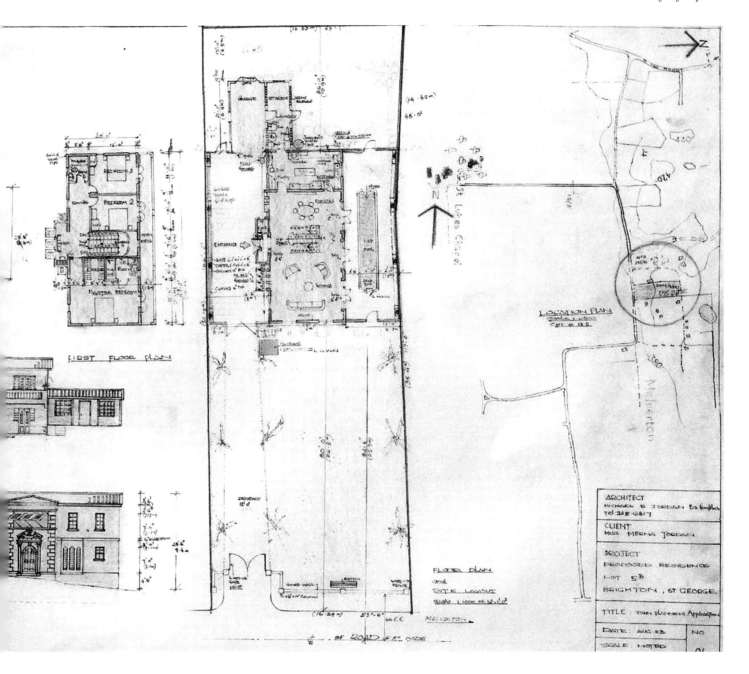

TCPO Application Plan

Interestingly, the entrance to the house was placed off this forecourt purposely not facing the street. We projected a two storey pediment as a visual architectural motif to signify entry to the public; but at the human scale an imposed pediment stressed the actual entrance leading into the lobby, setting a major axis to the grand imperial staircase which forms a double height space terminated with a high level elliptical window. This staircase is a reference from a house in London located at No. 44 Berkeley Square and which was once owned by Lady Isabella Finch. The staircase was designed and built by the celebrated British architect William Kent (1685-1748).

Hephizibah Staircase

In on the ground floor to the left of the minor axis is the kitchen, service area and the dining table. On the right flank is the living suite where three elliptical arched French doors screens the pool terrace. This single depth space positioned in the centre of the land creates space to the boundaries for the motor courtyard on the west side and the swimming pool and terrace walled in on the boundary forming another courtyard on the east. This device allows the living area space to extend into the courtyards creating indoor/outdoor space for private entertainment.

All bedrooms upstairs have all round views with a modest full length deck facing the east. Windows are French sash, block walls plastered and trowel plastic and the gable roof is zinc sheeting.

OTHER ARCHITECTURAL PROJECTS

<u>St. Thomas Secondary School (The Lester Vaughan School) 1992</u>

During the early 1990s, I got the opportunity to work at the education project office with Mr. H. B. Hunte and Mr. Pravin Patel on the proposed St. Thomas secondary school (now known as Lester Vaughan secondary school). At the time, they were completing the Queen's College secondary school in Husbands, St. Michael, and I got a head-start by assisting the architects with site supervision. I was able to use this information to assist with the program for the new school, which was almost similar but the new site at Cane Garden has different qualities.

Michael E. Jordan

The Lester Vaughn School

The requirements of the program had to be manipulated (the blocks were already designed) to suit this site. After an analysis of the space available, I decided to use the historical urban type of courtyard and atriums allowing the users of the surrounding wings to have their own courtyard.

This courtyard helps to control the airborne noises and the strong prevailing winds. Another design concept was to site the pavilion near the road to accommodate public use on weekends for cricket and football. Small buildings were then organized and arranged within a tight urban composition to form a network of pathways and courtyards. The importance and prominence of the hall and administration building is evident and readable in silhouette which is able to suit their use and function. It is evident from the past that building and urban types are universal due to human nature and it goes to reason that intelligence and beauty is eternal.

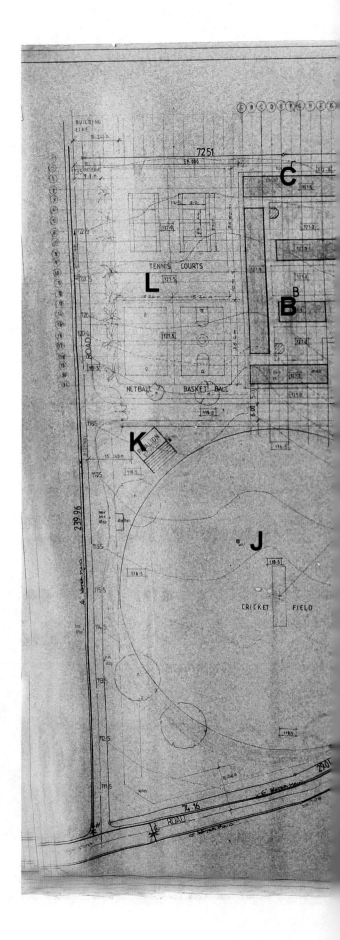

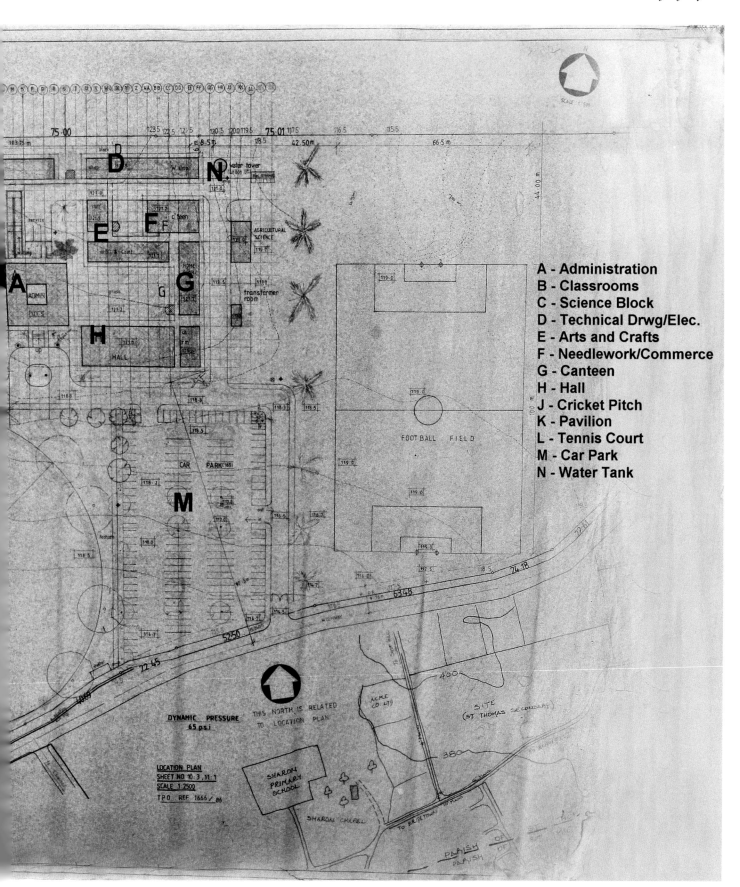

A - Administration
B - Classrooms
C - Science Block
D - Technical Drwg/Elec.
E - Arts and Crafts
F - Needlework/Commerce
G - Canteen
H - Hall
J - Cricket Pitch
K - Pavilion
L - Tennis Court
M - Car Park
N - Water Tank

Lester Vaughn School Site Plan

Conclusion

History is a collective experience, a group memory essential for the orientation of any people. Among the small fledging nations of the world today, many are still scarred from the colonial experience. The need for a positive reconstruction of the past is pressing, if for no other purpose than to provide them with a sense of direction in a chaotic world.

Barbados is still befuddled by the Expert Syndrome which often utilizes any imported talent for the solution of great problems, quite frequently at the expense of local expertise. More tragic than the colonial experience however had been the type of Plantation society created by the colonists.

Rather than adopt the negative view of plantation society, it is argued that our vernacular architecture is sufficiently vital as a distinct and valuable culture which is ours.

Architectural Design Course

After studying Architecture in London in the early 1980s, on his return to Barbados, the author decided to offer this course to assist locals in learning and benefiting from his knowledge and experience in this field and to empower persons who wished to enter this field. Thus, the benefits of studying this course would be:-

1. Preparing a portfolio to apply for university entry. (In order to register with the Barbados Institute of Architects, you need a University Degree outside of the Caribbean since there is currently no Architectural Degree Programme available in the region.)
2. Working locally in a hardware store
3. Preparing Town Planning applications as a draughtsman
4. Appreciation of Architecture
5. Attaining a job as a trainee draughtsman in an architect's office

Graduation Class of 2011

TECHNICAL EVENING INSTITUTE

The Technical Evening Institute is located at the corner of Nightengale Road, Black Rock, St, Michael.
Cell: (246) 245-6817
E-mail: micezjor60@hotmail.com
The institute offers a 6–12 month course - **Architectural Design**   (Theory of Classical Dream House Design and Tropical Architecture).

TABLE OF CONTENTS - <u>FROM THE TECHNICAL EVENING INSTITUTE BOOKLET</u>
GENERAL, AIMS, OBJECTIVES
ASSESSMENT, METHOD OF GRADING
ASSESSMENT SHEET
LECTURE TOPICS
DETAILED SYLLABUS
INSTRUMENTS FOR DESIGN COURSE
READING (MANDATORY & OPTIONAL)
ADMISSION
COURSE TUTORS

BOOKS AND TOOLS

MANDATORY

1. Architecture Drafting and Design – Hepler & Wallace
2. Draughtsmanship – Fraser Reekie
3. Creation of Lifestyle – Michael E. Jordan

Texts in the author's own library.

OPTIONAL (further reading)

1. Ways of Seeing – John Berger
2. Decoding Advertisements – Judith Williamson

TOOLS – Adj. set square, T-square, crayons, and rulers

ARCHITECTURAL DESIGN COURSE

1) GENERAL

The Certificate course in Architectural Design is being offered by the TECHNICAL EVENING INSTITUTE in conjunction with Michael Jordan Associates. It aims to assist in developing a greater appreciation for architecture, with emphasis in the area of theory of classical dream house design and tropical architecture, by using such elements as mythology, ideology and the imitation of nature.

2) AIMS

The Aims of the course are as follows:
a) To develop greater appreciation of architecture as a discipline.
b) To develop a "Thinking Being" (a person with the ability to analyse Architectural problems.)
c) To assist the public in Town Planning Applications (drawing plans).
d) To serve as a refresher course prior to International Training
(University Degree Programme)

ENTRY REQUIREMENTS
Age 16 +, 'O' level standard or a Mature student.

3) OBJECTIVES
At the end of the course, students will appreciate the Art of building and will make more meaningful contributions to the society in the creation of lifestyle and the environment in general.

MODULES OF THE COURSE

1. Orientation

Presentation by Michael Jordan – What is Architecture?, course outline, how to study, books/equipment, and the assessment

2. Geometrical Drawings

GEOMETRICAL DRAWING COURSE

(see Appendix for respective Geometrical Drawings figures)

(1) LINE TYPES (hidden lines. c/l, layout, finish, dimensions, lettering)

(2) CIRCLES

(3) ELLIPSE

(4) NEAR & FAR (Rendering)

(5) PROPORTION (The Virtruvian man)

(6) NATURE & GEOMETRY

(7) LIGHT & SHADE

(8) POLYGONS

(9) PERSPECTIVE

(10) TYPOLOGY

3. Site Planning

1. Positive/Negative Space
2. Streets and Piazza
3. Typology of city design – Greek, Roman, American
4. Jargon – Hard/Soft Edge
5. Site Appraisal – 11 Points
6. TCPO/MOH Regs

7. Indoor/Outdoor landscape space
8. Monumental Planning – Setback
9. Polar System – Perspective Space on The Acropolis, Greece
10. Inner City Gentrification - height, colour, edge, façade
11. Future extension – parking, etc.

4. History of Ideas – (An introduction to ideology)

1. Enlightenment Empiricism – Immanuel Kant (1724–1804)
2. Historical Idealism – G. W. F. Hegel (1770-1831)
3. Romanticism – Nietzsche (1804-1900)
4. Phenomenological Aesthetics – Martin Heidegger
5. Historical Materialism (Marxist Aesthetics) – Karl Marx (1818-1883)
6. Structuralism & the Epistemology of the sign – Claude Levi-Strauss (1908)

5. Design
PALLADIO VS. LE CORBUSIER
SITE APPRAISAL – 1. Budget, 2. Lifestyle, 3. Breeze direction, 4. Sunrise/Sunset, 5. Accommodation, 6. Soil depth, 7. Parking, 8. TCPO/MOH Building codes, 9. TOPO., 10. Best view, 11. Context

6. Integrated Technical Studies
Integrating Services – Structure, Electrical, Plumbing, Telephone

7. E.S.C.O.B. – Economics and Social Conditions of Building
Human Relations, Building cost and quantities and Types of construction

8. Glossary
JARGON – The language of Architecture

4) ASSESSMENT

Examinations for the course will take the form of continuous assessment leading to final grading.

The Examination Board will consist of the course leader and two external examiners.

5) METHOD OF GRADING

Grades are determined as follows:

10, 9:   A - Very Good

8, 7:   B - Good

6, 5:   C - Average

0   O – No Submission

TECHNICAL EVENING INSTITUTE
EXAMINER'S REPORT

Assessment	Floor Plan	Elevation	Site Plan	Interior Perspective	Cross Section	Misc. Sheet	Folio/ Essay	Oral	Visual	Research	**Pass Grade**

Date.........................

Signature...................................

Distinction / A+ -: 95-100

A   -: 85-95

B+ -: 75-85

B   -: 65-75

C   -: 50–65

Best Student must be present (except due to illness)

Bibliography

Beckford, George L. ***Persistent Poverty****: Underdevelopment in Plantation Economics of the Third World*, Oxford University Press, New York, 1972

Fraser, Henry S. ***Treasures of Barbados***, MacMillan Education Ltd., London, 1990

Porphyrios, Demetri (guest editor). ***Classicism Is Not A Style*** *(Architectural Design Magazine)*, London, 1982

Ramsey, Stanley C. & Harvey, J. D. M. ***Small Georgian Houses and their details*** *(1750 – 1820)*, Architectural Press, London, 1972

Reekie, Fraser. ***Draughtsmanship****: Architectural and Building Graphics*, 3rd edn, Edward Arnold (Publishers) Ltd., London, 1976

Snodin, Michael (editor). ***Karl Friedrich Schinkel****: A Universal Man*, Yale University Press with the Victoria and Albert Museum, New Haven and London, 1991

Wittkower, Rudolf. ***Architectural Principles in the Age of Humanism***, 4th edn, Academy Editions, London, 1973

Glossary of Terms

ARCHITRAVE: a curved or stepped *profile* to create the separation between two different *materials* (e.g. the wall, window or door frame)

BAJAN: an abbreviation for 'Barbadian' (local slang)

BAJAN CHATTEL HOUSE: a rectangular timber chattel house with one roof usually built on stone or concrete blocks

BAJAN VERNACULAR HOUSE: usually a timber house comprising of three hip/gable roofs with jalousie doors, windows and hoods

BAY: considered the width of a house no more than 20 feet

CAPITAL: considered the flanged top of a column

COLUMN
- **IONIC:** where the capital is fashioned similar to a ram's horn
- **DORIC:** where the capital is fashioned with three flanges
- **CORINTHIAN:** where the capital is fashioned similar to a wreath of flowers or leaves

CORNICE: the coping piece, usually at the top of a wall, with a wider profile used to shelter the wall from the weather

FAÇADE: the front view/elevation of a structure

FRIEZE: the section between the architrave and the cornice

GEORGIAN: an architectural style based on the Palladian system of harmony of balance, composition and symmetry which was introduced in England during the reign of the British kings George I, George II and Georgian III.

JALOUSIE
- **WINDOW:** usually built with top half, top-hung and bottom half, side-hung; fixed timber louvers to keep out rain and sun, but let in air and modest light
- **DOOR:** usually built in two halves; bottom panelled with adjustable louvers and sometimes a fixed glass panel at the top

LOAD-BEARING: consists of walls formed in block work without columns or posts

MOTIF: a theme/style articulated in architectural design from a given period/era

PEDIMENT: usually triangular, it consists of the *architrave* (stepped *profile* between the capital and the beam), the *frieze* (the beam separating the triangular, curved or stepped portion from the stepped profile) and the *cornice* (the top part of the beam, usually triangular, curved or stepped).

PLAN
- **SINGLE-BAY:** a typology or floor plan comprising of one *bay*
- **TWO-BAY:** plan consisting of two bays separated by either a column or wall partition
- **THREE-BAY:** plan comprising of three bays separated by columns or wall partitions

POST AND LINTEL: a construction where the column (post) supports a concrete or timber/wooden beam (lintel)

ROOF
- **GABLE:** a triangular roof constructed to slope in two directions from the centre
- **HIP:** a roof constructed to slope in four directions from a central point
- **LEAN-TO (SHED ROOF):** constructed to slop in one direction
- **PARAPET:** an overhanging roof cut off by the extension of external walls

TYPOLOGY: the geometrical footprint of a plan

VERANDA(H): usually an entrance room surrounded on three sides by jalousie louvers and doors.

Appendix

Photographs by Felix Kerr
Plans by Michael E. Jordan

Map of Barbados/Caribbean
The Barbados Museum & Historical Society
St. Nicholas Abbey
Drax Hall
Farley Hill
Table 1: Similar Lifestyles–Similar Plans–Varied Social Levels
Forde House
Bajan Chattel House
Home in Carmichael Heights, St. George (1986)
- Front/Back Elevation
- Ground Floor Plan
- Altes Museum (ref.)
- The Entrance Hall
'HAZA': A Home in St. Thomas
- West Elevation
- Ground Floor Plan
- Long Section
- The Hall
- Site Plan
'HEPHZIBAH': A Home in St. George (2001)
- Front Elevation (showing seven benefits)
- TCPO Application Plan
The Lester Vaughn School [formerly St. Thomas Secondary School] (1992)
- Photograph
- Site Plan
Technical Evening Institute's Graduating Class of 2011
Technical Evening Institute's Examiner's Report (specimen)
Geometrical Drawings
- Linetypes
- Circles
- Ellipse
- Near & Far
- Proportion
- Nature & Geometry
- Light & Shade
- Polygons
- Perspective
- Typology
Table 2: Process and Procedure

1. LINETYPES

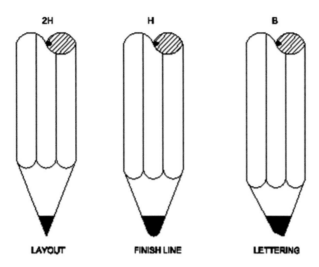

Figure 1: LETTERING

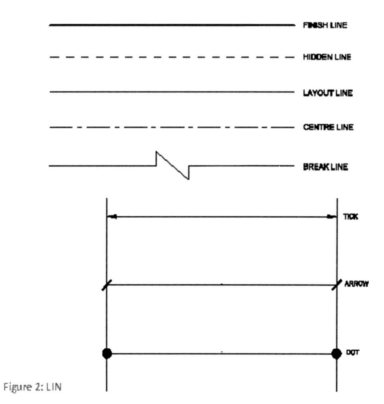

Figure 2: LIN

2. CIRCLE

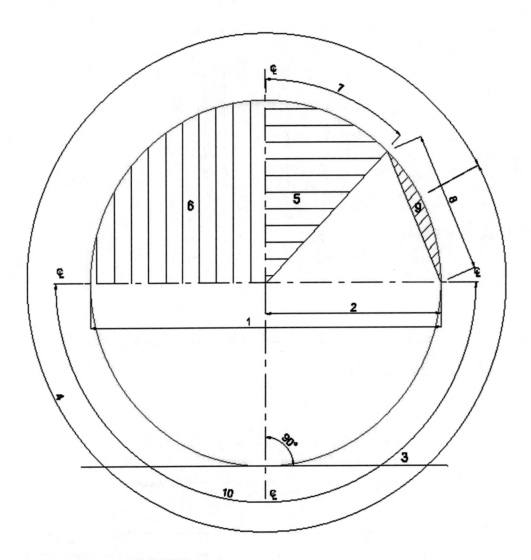

Figure 4: PARTS OF A CIRCLE

Parts of the Circle (Figure 4):
1. Diameter
2. Radius
3. Tangent
4. Circumference
5. Sector
6. Quadrant
7. Arc
8. Chord
9. Segment
10. Semi-circle

3. ELLIPSE

Method of Construction

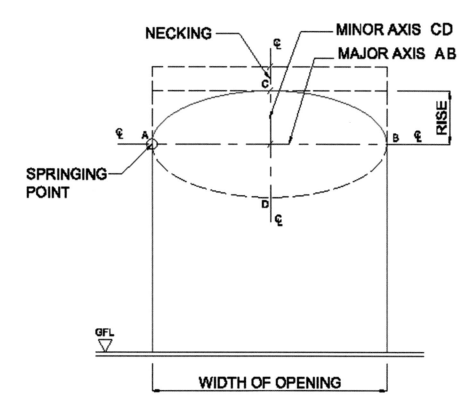

Figure 5: Ellipse Application in Arch Opening

Applications (Figure 5):
- Gardens/Windows/Doors
- Landscaping
- Stairwells
- Arches

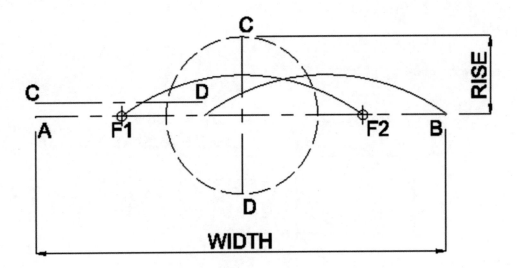

Figure 6: Ellipse Parameters

Method of Finding Ellipse Focal
Points F1 & F2 (Figure 6)

- Subtract CD from AB

- **The remainder is the distance
  between F1 & F2.**

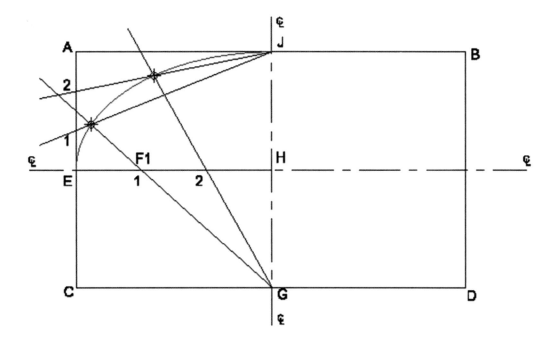

Figure 7: Ellipse Construction

Steps for Ellipse Construction (Figure 7):

1. Divide EH into 3 parts.
2. Divide EA into 3 parts
3. Draw through G1 and G2, J1 and J2. Draw the ellipse quadrant through the points where the lines cross

4. NEAR AND FAR

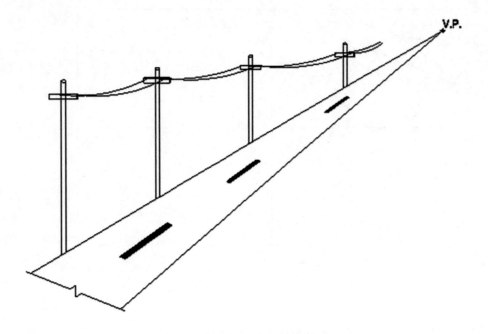

Figure 8: NEAR AND FAR

5.PROPORTION

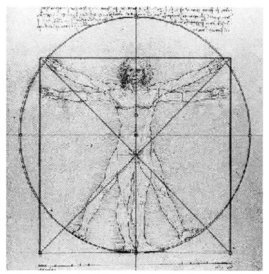

Figure 9: The Vitruvian Man approximates the Square

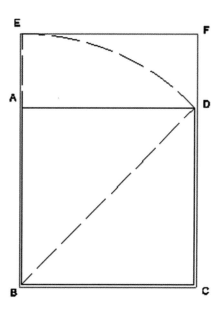

Figure 10: GOLDEN SECTION

Figure 11: VITRUVIAN MAN APPROXIMATES THE SQUARE

Steps for Golden Section Construction (Figure 9):
1. Draw square 'ABCD'
2. Rabat 'BD' to locate point 'E'
3. 'BCFE' forms the Golden Rectangle

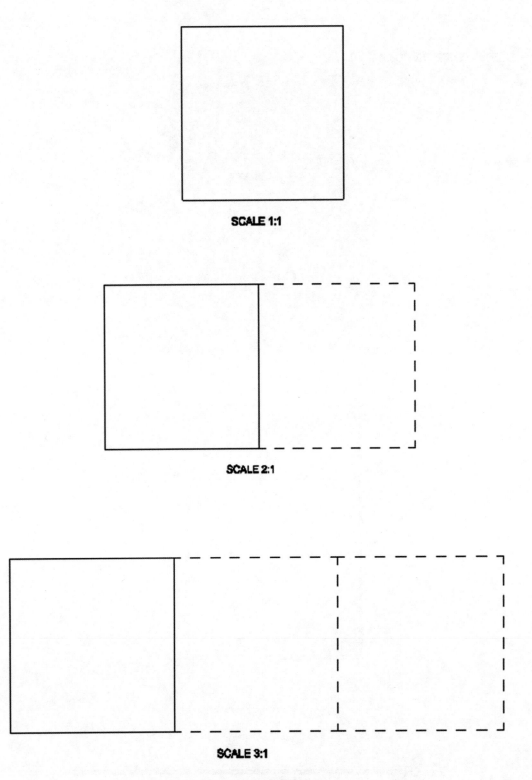

Figure 12: Scaled Objects

6. NATURE AND GEOMETRY

Figure 13: PENTAGONAL CROSS-SECTION OF OKRAS

Figure 14: PENTAGONAL CROSS-SECTION OF POMEGRANATE

7. LIGHT AND SHADE

Figure 15: SHADE ON BOX

Figure 166: SHADE ON CYLINDER

Figure 17: SHADE ON AN EGG-SHAPE

8. POLYGONS (SHAPES WITH MORE THAN 4 REGULAR SIDES)

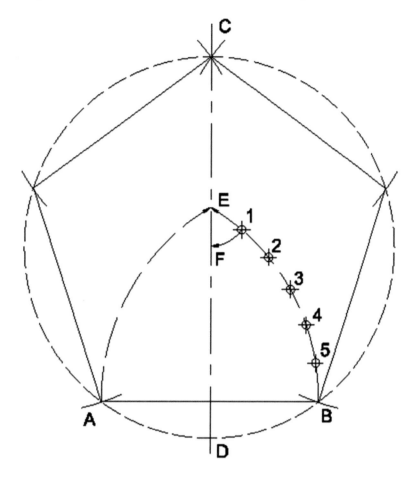

Figure 18: Pentagon Construction

Steps for Pentagon Construction (Figure 18):
1. Draw side 'AB'
2. Draw centreline 'CD'
3. Rabat 'A' and 'B' to get 'E'
4. Divide 'EB' into 6 parts
5. Rabat 'E1' to cut centreline at 'F' at the circle's centre
6. Draw circle
7. Using dividers with side 'AB', mark off the other sides of the pentagon

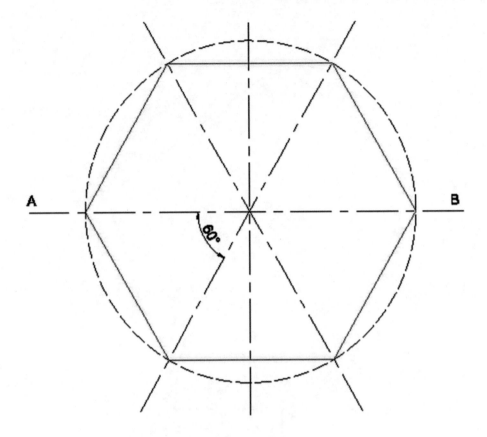

Figure 19: Hexagon Construction

Steps for Hexagon Construction (Figure 19):
1. Draw circle
2. Draw centreline on line 'AB'
3. Use 60° to get the other points

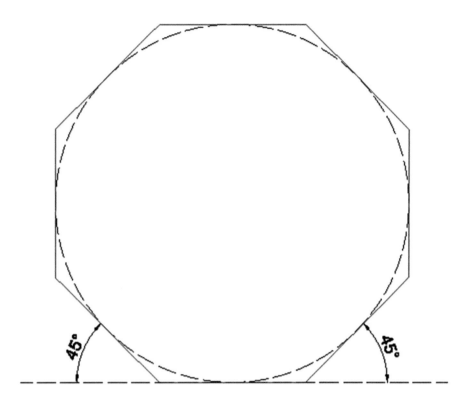

Figure 20: Octagon Construction

Steps for Octagon Construction (Figure 20):
1. Draw circle
2. Draw horizontal lines tangentially at the bottom and top of the circle
3. Draw vertical lines tangentially at the sides of the circle
4. Draw lines tangentially at 45° to join the horizontal and vertical line.

9. PERSPECTIVE

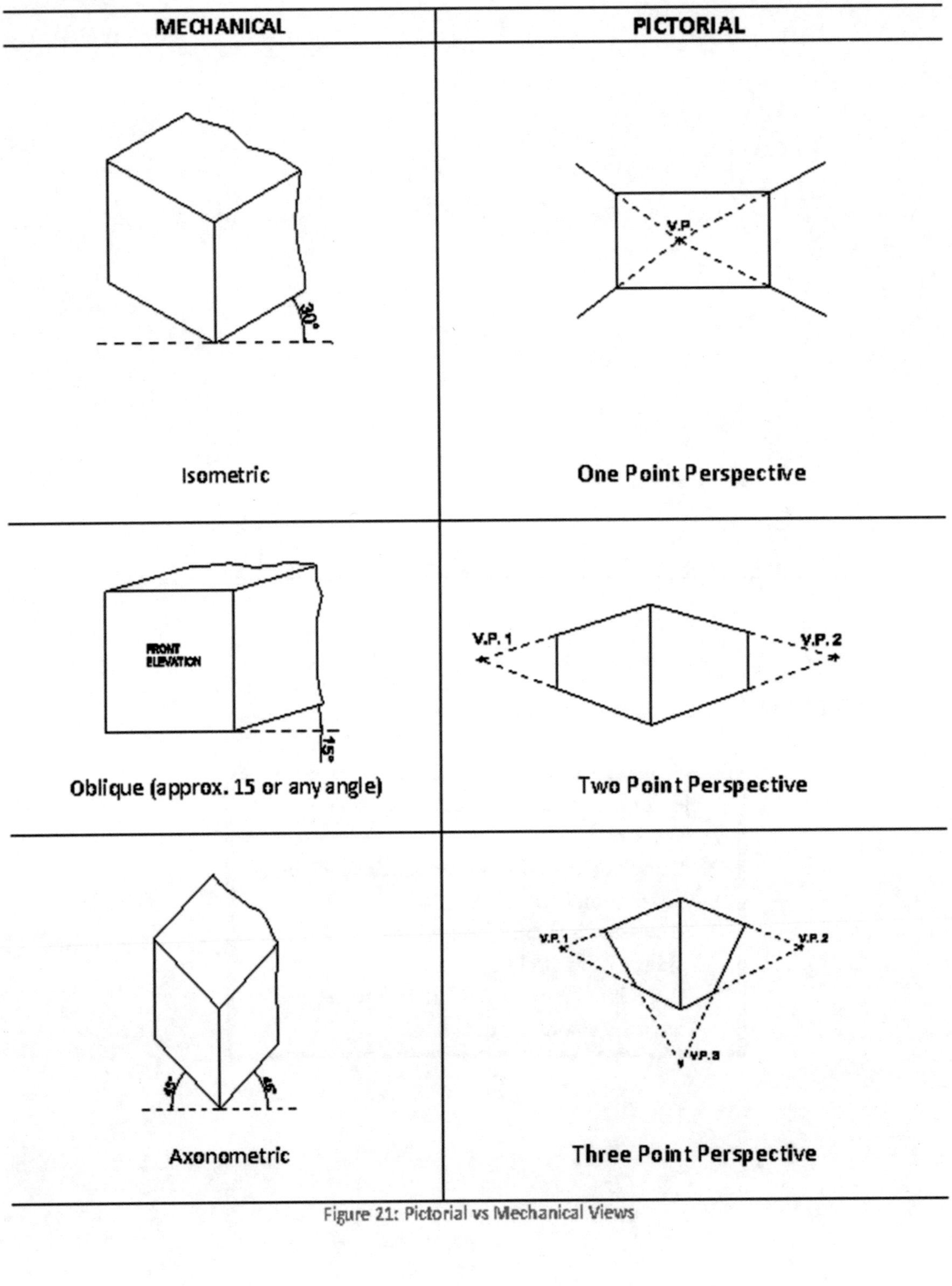

MECHANICAL
PICTORIAL
30°
Isometric
V.P.
One Point Perspective
FRONT ELEVATION
15°
Oblique (approx. 15 or any angle)
V.P. 1
V.P. 2
Two Point Perspective
45°
45°
Axonometric
V.P. 1
V.P. 2
V.P. 3
Three Point Perspective

Figure 21: Pictorial vs Mechanical Views

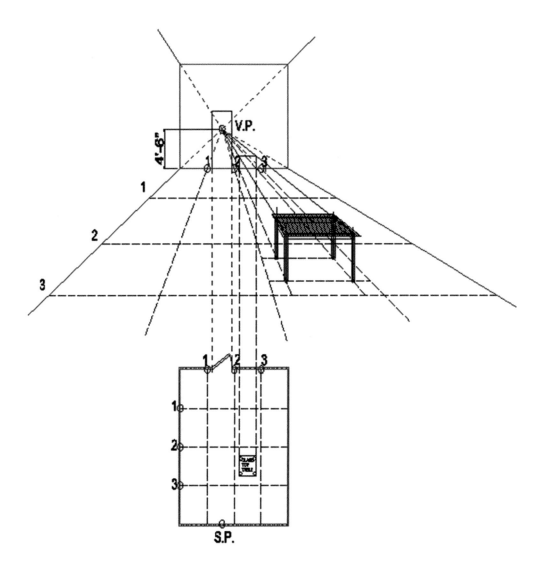

Figure 22: One Point Perspective Drawing

Perspective Drawing (Figure 22):

Method of One-Point Perspective: 16'x16' Room (By Author)

1. Draw the back wall elevation to ¼" scale
2. Establish station point (SP) on the plan
3. Establish vanishing point (VP) at 4'-6" above grade
4. Draw perspective line through the corners of the room
5. Tile the plan with 4'x4' tiles
6. By trial and error, put tiles in perspective on the corner lines of the room (each tile will get bigger as it gets nearer to the viewer)
7. As an example, put in a table on tile 3.3. First put the table on the back elevation (to scale) and project from the VP into the picture

10. TYPOLOGY

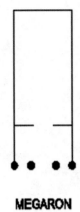

MEGARON

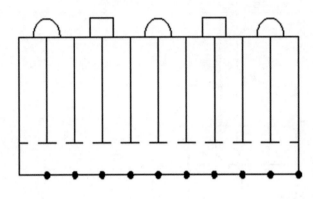

STOA

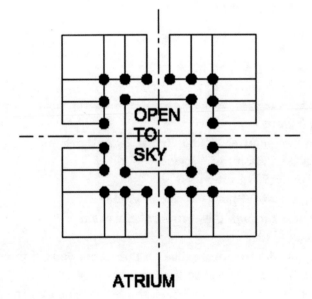

OPEN
TO
SKY

ATRIUM

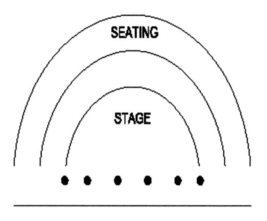

THEATRE

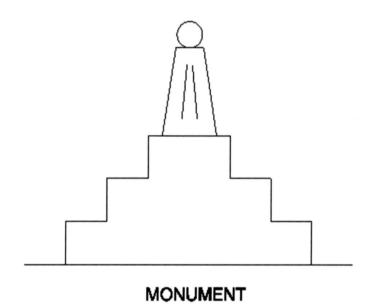

MONUMENT

TABLE 2: PROCESS AND PROCEDURE

REASONS	STAGES	SERVICE	FEE %	TIME (MNTHS)
• To know Architect • Architect to know the client	Inception	<u>Brief</u> – design a 3 bed/2 bath house to cost $500,000; lifestyle - a weekend retreat	0.5	1

• To get best decision
• Client to know the best design (based on facts)
	Sketch	<u>Site Appraisal:</u>
		   1. Budget
		   2. Lifestyle
		   3. Breeze direction
		   4. Sunrise/Sunset
		   5. Accommodation
		   6. Soil depth
		   7. Parking
		   8. TCPO/MOH Building codes
		   9. Topography.
		   10. Best view
		   11. Context
			1.5	1

• Government approvals • B.I.W.A. Connection	Town Planning Application	6 sets of plans, $100 application fee, plot, application form	2	6
• To get tenders • To give contract information	Working Drawings (Details)	Approx. 20 sheets e.g. electrical, roof, cupboards, etc.	3	2
• Least cost • Part of the Contract	Tenders	Contracts & Prices	1	1

• Avoid disputes
• Finish on time
	Site Supervision	Monthly site visits:
		   1.Quality
		   2.Payments
		   3.Progress
			2	6-12

TOTAL			10	24 (2 yrs.)

Portfolios of My Work (1974-Present)

1974 – 1980

FOLIO 1

St. Matthias, Christ Church
Lot 1 Wilcox Hill, Christ Church
Lot 11 Birds River Ave., Deacons Rd, St. Michael
Westbury Rd., St. Michael
Lot 4 Chancery Lane, Christ Church
Lot 58 Prior Park, St. James
Lot 31 Ealing Park, Stage 4, Christ Church
Lot 152 Bagatelle, St. James
Lot 118 Bagatelle, St. James
Lot 106 Enterprise, Christ Church
Lot 124 Bagatelle, St. James
Lower Fordes Rd. Clapham, St. Michael
Lot 7 St. Stephens Hill, St. Michael
31 Edgehill Heights, St. Thomas
Lot 5 Cave Hill, St. Thomas
Lot 13 Water Hall Terrace, St. James
Cave Hill, St. Michael
Lot 49 Goodland, Christ Church
Lot 36 Maycocks Bay, St. Lucy
Lot 22 Union, St. Philip
Lot 4 Paddock Rd., St. Michael
Durants Village, Christ Church
Lot 30 & 31 Railway Rd., St. Michael
Lot 5 Mangrove, St. Philip
Lot 1 Club Morgan, Christ Church
Goodland, St. Michael
Gemswick, St. Philip
Jackson, St. Michael

FOLIO 2

Lot 34 Bagatelle, St. James
Lot 80 Crane, St. Philip
Jubilee Gap, Peterkins Rd. Bank Hall, St. Michael
Arthur Seat, St. Thomas
Lot 24 Prospect, St. James
Lot 3 Friendly Hall, St. Philip
Lot 34 Husbands, St. James
Lower Civilian Rd. Spooners Hill, St. Michael
Lot 47 Jackson Stage 1, St. Michael
Boscobelle, St. Lucy
Lot 90 Wanstead, Cave Hill, St. Michael
Lot 16 Risk, St. James
Hastings, Christ Church
Apes Hill Tenantry, Orange Hill, St. James
Lot 38 Rock Dundo, St. James
Lot 72 Trents, St. James

FOLIO 3

Lot 51 Cane Garden, St. Michael
Lot 185 Bagatelle, St. James
Dayrells Rd., Christ Church
James Town Park, Holetown, St. James
Lot 26 Pine Rd., St. Michael
Lot 86 Water Hall Terrace, Section 2, St. Michael
Lot 4 Wavell Ave., Black Rock, St. Michael
Bagatelle, St. James
Lot 16 Bagatelle, St. James
Lot 6 Cane Garden, St. Michael
Lot 17 Atlantic Shores, Christ Church
Lot 2 White Hall, St. Michael
East Point, St. Philip
Rouen Radcot, St. Michael
Lot 29 Wavel Ave., Black Rock, St. Michael
Lot 9 & 10 Frere Pilgrim, Christ Church
Applegrove, Black Rock, St. Michael
Lot 75 Bagatelle, St. James

FOLIO 4

Lot 25 Silver Hill Drive, Christ Church
Chelsea Gardens, St. Michael
Lot 129 Long Ford Place, Waterford, St. Michael
1st Ave North Friendship Drive, Eden Lodge, St. Michael
Battaleys Plantation, St. Peter
Lot 63 Long Gap Grazettes, St. Michael
Bush Hall, St. Michael
Maxwell Main Rd., Christ Church
Lot 72 Rowans Park, St. George
Lot & Lot 23 Coverley, Christ Church
Quarry Rd., Bank Hall, St. Michael
Fitts Village, St. James
Lot 51 Eden Lodge, St. Michael
Lot 65 & Lot 67 Roebuck Street, St. Michael

FOLIO 5

Fairholme Gardens, Christ Church
Spring Hall Rural Development
No.66 Roebuck Street, St. Michael
Lot 86 Wanstead Heights, St. James
Holligan Rd., Bank Hall, St. Michael
Review Rd., Bush Hall, St. Michael
1st Ave. Beckles Hill, St.Michael
Mount Joy Ave., Pine, St. Michael
Mayers Rd., St. Michael
Westbury Rd., St. Michael
Village, St. James
Lot 20 Cane Garden, St. James
Reece Rd., St. Michael
Lot 65 Appleby Gardens, St. James
Lot 9 St. Stephens Hill, Black Rock, St. Michael

Lot 9 & 10 Frere Pilgrim, Christ Church
Lot 5 Rollins Rd. Christ Church
Lot 112 Cane Garden, Christ Church
Lot 18 Ruby, St. Philip
Bushy Park, St. Philip
Bush Hall, St. Michael
Gall Hill, Christ Church
Eagle Hall, St. Michael
Bartletts Tenantry Rd., Christ Church
Fitts Village, St. James
Hoytes Village, St. James
Water Street, Christ Church
Church Hill Rd., Ashton Hall, St. Peter
Gooding Rd. St. Stephens Hill, Black Rock, St. Michael
Brewster Rd. Barbarees Hill, St. Michael
Sandy Lane, St. James
Salters, St. George
Beaugeste Farm, Lot 7 The Hope, St. George
Tudor Bridge, St. Michael
Lot 5 Piedmont Park, Grazettes, St. Michael
Country Rd., St. Michael
Wanstead Heights, St. James
(Sign Board) Cnr. Trafalgar Square
Lot 4 2nd Ave. Harts Gap, Christ Church
Lot 53 Reece Rd. St. Michael
Bank Hall, St. Michael
Mayers Rd. My Lords Hill, St. Michael
"L. A Traitt" Black Rock, St. Michael
Fustic Village, St. Lucy
Greaves Rd. Westmoreland, St. James
St. Lawrence Gap, Christ Church
Butlers Ave. Spooners Hill, St. Michael
Foster Hall, St. John
Lot 54 Gibbons, Christ Church
Suttle Street, St. Michael
9th Ave. Belleville, St. Michael
Rock Hall, St. John
Lot 58 Halton St. Philip
Newton Terrace, Christ Church
Cane Vale, Christ Church
Lot 20 Cane Garden, St. Thomas
Black Rock, St. Michael
Light Foot Lane, The City, St. Michael
Wildey Terrace, St. Michael
Montrose, Christ Church
Henry's Lane, Bay Street, St. Michael
Lukes Ave Beckles Rd., St. Michael
Spooners Hill, St. Michael
St. Stephens Hill, Black Rock, St. Michael
Ashton Hall, St. Peter
Lot 14 Bayfield, St. Philip

Michael E. Jordan

FOLIO 6

Lot 45 Mullins, St. Peter
Sargeants Village, Christ Church
Lot 5 Black Rock, Nr. Carlton, St. Michael
Lot 1 Ealing Park, Christ Church
Lot 118 Sec. 2 Rowans Park, St. George
Lot 53 Bagatelle, St. James
Martindale Rd., St. Michael
1st Ave. Wildey Terrace, St. Michael
Government Hill, St. Michael
North Friendship Drive, St. Michael
Cleavers Hill, Bathsheba, St. Joseph
Lot 13 Heddings, St. Philip
Lot 14 Coles, St. Philip
Wanstead St. James
Thornbury Hill, Christ Church
Nelson Street, St. Michael
Lot 54 Kingsland Terrace, Christ Church
Lot 71 Maynards, St. Peter
Laynes Rd., St. James
Resevoir Rd. Brittons Hill, St. Michael
Lot 4 Lower Burney, St. Michael
1st Ave. Pine Plantation Rd., St. Michael
Burkes Rd. Brittons Hill, St. Michael
Christ Church
Lot 49 Cane Wood Rd. Jackson, St. Michael
Subdivision into lots
Lot 26 The Valley, Nr. Charles Rowe Bridge, St. George
Greenidges, St. Lucy
Lot 22 Enterprise, Christ Church
Pine Industrial Estate

FOLIO 7

Lot 125 St. Barnabas Landing Scheme, St. Michael
Dover, Christ Church
Lot 58 Eden Lodge, St. Michael
Lot 63 Long Gap Grazettes, St. Michael
Lot 15 Newton Terrace, Christ Church
Barbarees Hill (Philips Site)
Cane Garden, St. Thomas
Lot 12 John's Plain, St. James
Holders Hill, St. James
Porters Rd., St. Peter
Lot 19 & 20 1st Ave. Jones Land, Black Rock, St. Michael
Lot 134 Grazettes, St. Michael
Grants Gap, Westbury Rd., St. Michael
Gully Field Ave. Bay Land, Beckles Road, St. Michael
St. Philip
Lot 12 Ealing Grove, Christ Church
Lot 20 Atlantic Shores, Christ Church
Kendall Hill, Christ Church

FOLIO 8

Melverton, St. George
Lot 29 Crane Haven, St. Philip
Chancery Lane, Christ Church
Lot 3 Wildey Terrace, St. Michael
Lot 64 Welches St. Thomas
Lot 43 Rock Dundo Park, St. Michael
3rd Ave Strathclyde, St. Michael
Lot 60 Stage 1, Christ Church
Chapman Lane, City, St.Michael
Lot 11 Newton, Christ Church
Lot 37 Goodland, Christ Church
Lot 204 Ruby, St. Philip
Lot 27 Durants, Christ Church
Dayrells Rd., Christ Church
1st Ave. Bank Hall, St. Michael
Lot 11 Birds River Ave., Deacons Rd., St. Michael - For Asley Gooding
Lot 9 Club Morgan, Christ Church
Lot 48 Kendall Hill, Christ Church
Lot 175 Long Bay, St. Philip
Lot 16 Bagatelle, St. James
Lot 7 CleveldaleRd. Black Rock, St. Michael
Lot 39 & Lot 40 1st Ave. Grazettes, St. Michael
Lot 23 Wavel Gardens, Black Rock, St. Michael
Lot 118 Warrens, St. Thomas
Lot 119 Water Hall Terrace, St. James
Lot 53 Warrens, St. Michael
Coffee Gully, St. Joseph
Lot 70 Sheraton Park, Christ Church
Hood Rd. Christ Church
Carmichael Heights, St. George
Rouens, St. Michael

FOLIO 9

Ealing Park, Christ Church
Lot 84 Water Hall Terrace, Christ Church
Richmond Black Rock, St. Michael
Waterford, St. Michael
Lake Close, Eden Lodge, St. Michael
Lot 94 Wanstead, St. Michael
Lot 91 Husbands, St. James
Lot 32 Rowans, St. George
Lot 19 White Hall, St. Michael
Foster Lodge, St. George
(Proposed cottage) Clapham, Christ Church
Chancery Lane, Christ Church
Foul Bay, St. Philip
Lot 23 South Hampton Ave., Cave Hill, St. Michael
Lot 24 Rowans, St. George
Rock Hall, St. Lucy
Fairfield Rd. Black Rock, St. Michael
Lot 50 Mullins Terrace, St. Peter
Lot 72 Long Bay, St. Philip
Lot 86 New Orleans, St. Michael

Fairfield Rd. Black Rock, St. Michael
Roberts Rd., St. Michael
Lot 6 Friendly Hall, St. George
Lewis Gap, Green Hill, St. Michael

FOLIO 10

Sea Rocks, Enterprise, Christ Church
Passage Rd., St. Michael
Lot 114 Stage 2 Kingsland, Christ Church
Lot 10 Abbey, Christ Church
Ealing Park, Christ Church
Arthur Seat, St. Thomas
Sam Lord's Castle, St. Philip
Lot 2 Burkes Rd. Brittons Hill, St. Michael
Lot 10 Longford Place Waterford, St. Michael
Eckstein Village, Tudor Bridge, St. Michael
Lot 34 & 35 Sheraton Park, Christ Church
Mahica Gap, St. Michael
Lot 26 Jackson Terrace, St. Michael
Lot 19 Kingsland Terrace, Christ Church
2nd Ave Bank Hall, St. Michael
Monroe Rd., St. Michael
Lot 13 St. Paul's Ave. Beckles Rd., St. Michael
Jackmans, St. Michael
Lot 37 Kendall Hill, Christ Church
Lot 113 Jackson Terrace, Christ Church
Lot 36 Clermont Gardens, St. James
Fairfield Rd. Black Rock, St. Michael
Kingsland Stage 3, Christ Church
Tudor Street, St. Michael
Lot 294 Union, St. Philip
Lot 119 Cane Garden, St. Michael
Lot 15 Pegwell, Christ Church
Resevoir Rd. Lodge Hill, St. Michael
Lot 82 Maycocks Bay, St. Lucy
Lot 19 White Hall, St. Michael
Eagle Hall, St. Michael
James Street, Bridgetown, St. Michael
My Lords Hill, St. Michael
Lot 10 Sheraton Park, Christ Church
Workmans, St. George
St. Barnabas, St. Michael

FOLIO 11

King Edward Rd. Bank Hall, St. Michael
Cave Hill, St. Michael
Holetown, St. James
Lot 11 Crane, St. Philip
Maycocks Bay, St. Lucy
Near Sun Valley, St. James
Brandons, St. Michael
Lot 18 Eden Lodge, St. Michael
Lot 110 Wanstead Heights, St. Michael

Lakes Folly, The City, St. Michael
Lot 59 Kendal Hill, Christ Church
Lot 26 Fairholme Gardens, Christ Church
Amity Lodge, Christ Church
Black Rock Nr. Paradise, St. Michael
Blowers, St. James
Dover Gardens, Christ Church

FOLIO 12

Rockley New Rd., Christ Church
Lot 9 Ellis Development, Fairfield Rd. Black Rock, St. Michael
Bank Hall Main Rd., St. Michael
Cane Vale Rd., Christ Church
Belmont Rd., St. Michael
Lot 17 Atlantic Shores, Christ Church
Lot 27 Water Hall Terrace, St. Michael
East Point, St. Philip
Hinds Hill, Cave Hill, St. Michael
Railway Track, Barkers Rd., St. Michael
Cane Vale, Christ Church
Lot 13 Kingsland, Christ Church
Baxters Rd., St. Michael
Maxwell Hill, Christ Church
Lot 22 Wilcox, Christ Church
Lot 132 Waterford, St. Michael
Westbury Rd., St. Michael
Lot 72 Harmony Hall, St. Philip
Lot 24 Gibbons, Christ Church
Lot 94 Cane Garden, St. Michael
Nelson Street, St. Michael
Lot 22 Newton Stage 11, Christ Church
Lot 81 Prior Park, Christ Church
Elizabeth Park, Christ Church
Lot 24 Elizabeth Park, Christ Church
Pile Bay, Spring Garden, St. Michael
Lot 6A The Glebe, St. George
Lot 7 Kendal Hill, Christ Church

U. K. CLIENTS (1981 – 1989)

Lot 444 Ruby, St. Philip
Lot 28 Halton, St. Philip
Lot 23 The Rock, St. Peter
Lot 1 Monroe Rd. Haggatt Hall, St. Michael
Lot 198 Palm Court Stage 3, Fortescue, St. Philip
No. 52 Tottenham U.K
Shop Hill, St. Thomas
Lot 52 The Rock, St. Peter
Lot 66 The Rock, St. Peter
Lot 128 Atlantic Shores, Christ Church
Welchman Hall, St. Thomas
Lot 30 The Rock, St. Peter
Lot 53 The Rock, St.Peter

Michael E. Jordan

YEAR OUT (1985)

James Street, Bridgetown, St. Michael
Smith Rd. Fairfield, Black Rock, St. Michael
Lot 1 Bagatelle, St. Thomas
Lot 93 Maynards, St. Peter
Spring Garden, Nr. Paradise, St. Michael
Emmerton Lane, City, St. Michael
Eastlyn, St. George
Regency Park, Christ Church
Ocean View Rd. Spooners Hill, St. Michael
Sewer Construction, Bay Street, St. Michael
Rock Dundo, St. James
Taylors Gap & Barbarees Hill, St. Michael
Regency Park, Christ Church
Bay Woods, St. James
Lot 3 Mullins, St. Peter

1985

Mount All, St. Andrew
Mount All, St. Andrew
Pine, St. Michael
Tudor Bridge, St. Michael
Sea View, St. James
Church Hill, St. George
School Rd. Hindsbury Rd., St. Michael
Andrews Tenantry, St. Joseph
King Street, St. Michael
Ellerslie, Black Rock, St. Michael
Ruby, St. Philip
Blades Hill, St. Philip
No. 19 Trents, St. James

1986

Lashley Rd., St. James
Buckingham Rd. Bank Hall, St. Michael
Lot 5 Gibbs, St. George
Lodge Hill, St. Michael
Lot 147 Bagatelle, St. James
Lot 31 Cane Garden, St. Thomas
Dayrells Rd., St.Michael
Dunscome, St. Philip
Whitehall, St. Michael
59 Oxnards, St. James
67 Bagatelle, St. Thomas
Husbands, St. James
Diamond Valley, St. Philip
Lot 202 Olive Drive, Cave Hill, St. Michael
Tamarind Ave., Culloden Rd., St. Michael
Lammings, St. Joseph
Grazettes, St. Michael
Enterprise, Christ Church
Lot 9 Callenders, Christ Church

1987

JANUARY
12 Marleyvale, St. Philip
Lot 9 Callenders, Christ Church

FEBRUARY
Rendezvous, Christ Church
62 Callenders, Christ Church
Hinds Hill, Cave Hill, St. Michael

MARCH
Lot 3 Liverpool Development, Enterprise, Christ Church
White Hall, St. Michael

MAY
(Sand Dune) Silver Sands, Christ Church
41, 48, 49 Callenders, Christ Church

JUNE
Sandbox Ave. Chelsea, St. Michael

JULY
Brittons Cross Rd., St. Michael
68 Mangrove, St. Philip

SEPTEMBER
Bagatelle, St. James

NOVEMBER
Alleynes Lane, Passage Rd., St. Michael

PROJECTS – 1988

Lot 43 Bannatyne Gardens, Christ Church
Lot 46 Bannatyne Gardens
Lot 62 Bannatyne Gardens
Lot 91 Sanford, St. Philip
Rosehill, St. George
St. Thomas
Pegwell Gardens, Christ Church
Gibbs, St. Peter
Pine Gardens, St. Michael
Crab Hill, St. Lucy
Lot 146 Maycocks, St. Lucy
Queen Mary Rd., St. Michael
Maxwell Coast Rd., Christ Church

PROJECTS – 1989

Queen Mary Rd., St.Michael
Littleheath, The Garrison, St. Michael
Lot 185 Kingsland II, Christ Church

Michael E. Jordan

PROJECTS – 1990

Bannatyne Gardens, Christ Church
Bank Hall, St. Michael
Amity Lodge, Christ Church
Pegwell Gardens, Christ Church
Lot 744 Cherry Close, Ruby, St.Philip
Barracks Hill, St. Michael
The Mount, St. George
Passage Gardens, St. Michael
King St., St. Michael
Passage Gardens, St. Michael

PROJECTS – 1991

Lot 3 Enterprise, Christ Church
Long Gap, St. Michael
Ashford, St. John
Lot 15 Guinea, St. John
Rosehill, St. George
Marshall Hall, Church Village, St. Philip

PROJECTS – 1992

Lot 38 Canevale, Christ Church
Lot 8 Carmichael Heights, St. George
St. Judes Nursing Home, Holders Hill, St. James
Lot 1113 Kingsland, Christ Church
Lot 60 Bannatyne Gardens, Christ Church
Perry Gap, Roebuck Street, St. Michael
Free Hill, Black Rock St. Michael   (* Details)

PROJECTS – 1993

Lot 31 Durette Gardens, St. Philip
Lot 2 Appleby Gardens, St. James
Lot 13 Clerview Dr. Clermont, St. James
Wycliff, Enterprise, Ch. Ch. Ref. no. 1924/11/93Ddd.11- 02-94
Lot 1 Spring Garden, St. Michael
Edgehill, St. John
Ruby Development, St. Philip
Freehill, Black Rock, St. Michael
Eastland, St. George
Pebble Beach Hotel, St. Michael
Ashford, St. John
Rusher Village, Fisher Pond, St. Joseph

PROJECTS – 1994

Lot 13 Prior Park, St. James
Lot 14 Hanson Heights, St. George
Lot 75 Delia Walk, St. James
Lot C1 13 Graeme Hall Park, Christ Church

Lot 3 Appleby Gardens, St. James
Edghill, St. Thomas

PROJECTS – 1995

Lot 115 Oldbury Terrace, St. Philip
Chapel St. Speightstown, St. Peter
Clerpark, St. Thomas
Newbury Crescent, St. George
Bagatelle, St. Thomas
Lot 1014 Kingsland, Christ Church
Lot 100 Warrens Park South, St. Michael
Lot 1 Callenders, Christ Church
Lot 53 Husbands, St. Michael
Mapp Hill, St. John
Lot 1046 Kingsland, Christ Church
Lot 95 Palm Court, St. Philip

PROJECTS – 1996

Lot 1086 Kingsland Heights, Christ Church
Hunte Street, The City, St. Michael
Lot 13 White Hall, Cave Hill, St.Michael
St. Michael's Rowe, St. Michael
Yearwood Rd. Black Rock, St. Michael
Lot 30 East Winds, St. Philip
Lot 486 West Terrace, St. James
Lot 15 Gibbs Glade, St. Peter
Lot 9 11th Ave. Belleville, St. Michael
Lot 18 Welches, St. Thomas
Lot 2 Fresh Water Bay, Brighton, St. Michael
Lot 5 Fresh Water Bay, Brighton, St. Michael
Kingsland, Christ Church
Carrington Village, St. Michael
Rowans Park North, St. George
Stanmore Terrace, St. Michael

PROJECTS – 1997

Lot 2 Walkes Spring, St. Thomas
Valcluse, St. Thomas
St. Peter
Harbour Industrial Park
Passage Gardens, St. Michael
Welches, St. Thomas   (* Details)
Pine Industrial Park, St. Michael
Lot 78E Husbands Heights, St. Michael

RICES F.H. LTD - F.A.N. BOSTIC:
Lot 69 Husbands Heights, St.Michael
Lot 4 Harmony, St. Philip
Lot 1040 Kingsland, Christ Church
Lot 1066 Kingsland, Christ Church

Lot 7 Harmony, St. Philip
Lot 1026 Kingsland, Christ Church
Lot 18 Husbands Heights, St. Michael
Crane, St. Philip

PROJECTS: SEPT. –DEC. 1997

RICES F.H. LTD – F.A.N. BOSTIC:

Lot 5 Jackson, St. Michael
Husbands Crescent, St. Michael
Husbands Crescent, St. Michael
Lot C3/5 Graeme Hall Park, Christ Church
Lot 187 Wotton, Christ Church
Lot 71 Husbands Crescent, St. Michael
Lot 73 Husbands Crescent, St. Michael
Lot 5 Harmony Lodge, St. Philip
Lot 40 Husbands Heights, St. James
Lot 25 Sheraton Park, Christ Church
Lot 912 Kingsland Crescent, Christ Church
Lot 48 Harmony Lodge, St. Philip
Lot 4 Emerald Beach, St. James
Lot 6 Emerald Beach, St. James

PROJECTS: JAN. – APRIL 1998

RICES F.H. LTD – F.A.N. BOSTIC:

Lot 69 Husbands, St. James
Lot 5 Harmony Lodge Stage 2, St. Philip
Lot 317 Windward Gardens Phase 2, St. Philip
Lot 7 Briar Hall, Christ Church
Lot 7 Husbands Heights, St. James
Lot 454 Kingsland Terrace Stage 3, Christ Church
Lot 12 Gibbs, St. Peter
Lot 78 Husbands Crescent, St. James
Lot 8 Harmony Lodge, St. Philip

Lot 72 Crystal Heights, St. James
Lot 96 St. Silas Heights, St. James (sold to Terrance Howell)
Lot 2 Bartletts Tenantry, St. Michael
Lot 21 Warrens Heights, St. Michael
Lot 75 Union Park, St. Philip

PROJECTS: MAY – DEC. 1998

RICES F.H. LTD – F.A.N. BOSTIC:

Lot 11 Harmony, St. Philip
Lot 102 Crystal Heights, St. James
Lot 134 Husbands Heights, St. James
Lot 116 Crystal Heights, St. James
9th Ave. Belleville, St. Michael
Lot 148 Goodland Gardens, Christ Church
Lot 47 Warners, Christ Church

Jackman's, St. Michael
Lot 48 Green Point, St. Philip
Lot 2 Prospect, St. James   (* Details)
Crystal Heights, St. James
Lot 15 Bridgefield, St. Thomas
Gibbons, Christ Church
Lot 1A Arthur Seat, St. Thomas
3rd Friendship Terrace, St. Michael
Ashby Ave., Oistins, Christ Church
150 Bagatelle Terrace, St. James
Bridgefield, St. Thomas

PROJECTS: JAN. – DEC. 1999

Crumpton Street, The City
Lot 74 Appleby Gardens, St. James
Pilgrim Place, Christ Church
Lot 3 White Hall #1, St. Michael
Lot 44 Hartland Road, Haynesville, St. James
Lot 3 Carters Gap, Christ Church
Lot 1 Silver Sands, Christ Church
Kew Road, St. Michael
Lot 64 Sunset Heights, Maynards, St.Peter
Walkers #2 St. George
Gemswick, St. Philip
Derriston Rd. Garzettes, St. Michael
Lot 31 Husbands Heights, St. James

PROJECTS: JAN. – DEC. 2000

Airy Hill, St. George
Lot 25 & 26 Coverley Terrace, Christ Church
Lot 5 Fresh Water Bay, St. Michael
Lot 50 Trents, St. Lucy
Plumgrove, Christ Church
Lot 21 North Friendship, St. Michael
Maxwell Top Road, Christ Church
Lot 72 Husbands, St. James

PROJECTS: JAN. – MAY 2001

2 presentation pieces
Lot 1 Pie Corner, St. Lucy (Apt.)
Suttle Street, The City, St. Michael
Lot 1 Durants, Christ Church
Lot 55 Oxnards, St. James (2 basement apartments)
Salters, St. Michael
4th Ave. Peterkins Land, St. Michael
Cave Hill, St. Michael
Oxnards, St. James
Durette Gardens, St. Philip

Michael E. Jordan

FOLIO 2002

Nos

85	3rd Ave. Goddings Rd., St.
70	The Crane, St. Philip
	Graham Hall, Christ Church
	Fordes Road, Christ Church
91	

FOLIO 2003

	Crumpton St., Bridgetown, St. Michael (retention plan)
80	
92	Nr. Providence, Christ Church
	Off Lodge Road, Christ Church
93	
94	Lot 5D Brighton, St. George

FOLIO 2004

97	Kew Road, St. Michael	1364/05/04 A
98	The Kew Rd., St. Michael	2495/08/04
99		
100		
101	Appleby, St. James	
102	Bank Hall, St. Michael	3101/10/04 A, 1797/06/05 A
103	Lot 1 Newbury Crescent, St. George	
104	St. Silas Heights, St. James	
105	Galoway Rd., 129 Waterford, St. Michael	
106	Belfield, St. Michael	3837/12/04 A

FOLIO 2005

107		
108	St. Stephen's Hill, St. Michael	211/01/05/ A
109	Carlton, St. James	
110	Wavell Ave., Black Rock, St. Michael	0510/02/05
111	Sketch	
112	Lot 6 Clermont, St. Michael (proposed extension)	
113	213 Phineys, St. Philip	0213/0253/02/96 E
114	Greaves Hill, St. Philip	1893/06/05 E
115	Lot 15 Accomadation Road, St. Michael	1622/05/05 A
116	Bottom Bay, St. Philip	
117	Bottom Bay, St. Philip	
118	Bottom Bay, St. Philip	
119		
120	"Caladonia", St. Stephen's Hill, St.Michael	
121	(extension, rebasement) St. George	
122		
123	Bourne Village, St. George	3989/12/2005 B
124	Lot 152 Edghill, St. Thomas	3459/11/2005 C
125	Rockhampton Rd. Grazettes, St. Michael	
126	1st Ave. Sealy Land, Bank Hall, St. Michael	

127	Baycroft Rd. Bridge Road, St. Michael	106/04/2006 B
128	Andrews Tenantry, Parris Hill, St. Joseph	921/03/06 C
129	St. Stephen's Landing Scheme, St. Michael	
130	Lot 88 St. Patricks, Christ Church	2279/7/2006
131	Cnr. Nightengale, Blk Rd. St.Michael	
132	Tichbourne, St. Michael	2006/06/06 B
133	3rd Ave. Goodings Rd., Station Hill, St. Michael	3499/11/2006 A
134A		
134B		
135	Chalky Mount, St. Andrew	
136	Farm Rd., St. George	3565/11/06 B
137	Lot 4 Fairview, Christ Church	
138	Kensington, St. Michael	
139	St. Michael	
140	St. Michael	
152	Lot 41 Hothersal Tenantry, St. John	
153	Wanstead, St. Michael	
154	Accra, Christ Church	
155	15 C Eden Lodge, St. Michael	
156	305 Simmons Dev. Club Morgan, Christ Church	
157	St. Silas Heights, Christ Church	
158	Lot 13 Rices, St. Philip	2732/9/08
159	Cnr. Nightengale Gardens, Black Rock, St. Michael	
160	Tudor Bridge, St. Michael	
161	St. Margaret's Village, St. John	
162	Alleynedale, St.Lucy	

Printed in the United States
By Bookmasters